Grace Rediscovered

"In *Grace Rediscovered*, Ben Gosden leads us on a journey through fatigue, confusion and angst to God's gifts of grace, healing and hope. Ben is a spiritual guide whose life bears witness to authenticity and courage, and his ministry is an outward and visible sign of these virtues. This book is an extraordinary and timely resource for this season."

—Ken Carter, Bishop, The United Methodist Church and Consulting Faculty, Duke University Divinity School

"I don't know many clergy who haven't had an existential crisis in the past few years. Ben Gosden's book is a helpful resource for those who are in an existential crisis or want to create a ministry that is less likely to lead to one."

—Luke Edwards, author of *Becoming Church: A Trail Guide for Starting Fresh Expressions*

"The principles and practices of the twelve steps of recovery have been one source of healing in my life. For eight years I served in a congregation of 'hope dealers': former dope dealers, workaholics or convicts who were met by the resurrected Jesus (sometimes known by that name and other times known only by his signature of new life). Persons in twelve-step recovery have discipled me and offer the gift of wisdom to the church. Ben's vulnerable act of sharing his journey of recovery is a powerful example of that gift. Every chapter describes a principle of recovery along with practical tools to meet you in your journey. Be warned: following this path will be painful, but not a pain multiplied by shame. It will be the pain of growth and hope and new life. Find a few people to read this book with. Let's quit hiding our secrets and begin living in the Light."

—Melissa Maher, United Methodist pastor, Houston, Texas

"Ben Gosden has written a bold and courageous book that will help you in your spiritual growth. You will find in Gosden's writing an invitation to the deep work of transformation. He's done the hard work himself. His gift to us is that in *Grace Rediscovered* he describes the journey and serves as a trusted guide that models the way forward for the rest of us. Read it. Digest it. Live it. You'll be glad you did. Highly recommend."

—Brian Russell, professor of biblical studies, Asbury Theological Seminary

Grace Rediscovered

*Finding Hope and Healing Through
Faith and Recovery*

BY **Ben Gosden**

FOREWORD BY
Jorge Acevedo

WIPF & STOCK · Eugene, Oregon

GRACE REDISCOVERED
Finding Hope and Healing Through Faith and Recovery

Copyright © 2024 Ben Gosden. All rights reserved. Except for brief quotations in critical publications or reviews, no part of this book may be reproduced in any manner without prior written permission from the publisher. Write: Permissions, Wipf and Stock Publishers, 199 W. 8th Ave., Suite 3, Eugene, OR 97401.

Wipf & Stock
An Imprint of Wipf and Stock Publishers
199 W. 8th Ave., Suite 3
Eugene, OR 97401

www.wipfandstock.com

PAPERBACK ISBN: 979-8-3852-2747-1
HARDCOVER ISBN: 979-8-3852-2748-8
EBOOK ISBN: 979-8-3852-2748-8

Unless otherwise indicated, Scripture quotations are from New Revised Standard Version Bible, copyright © 1989 National Council of the Churches of Christ in the United States of America. Used by permission. All rights reserved worldwide.

Scripture quotations marked (NIV) are taken from the Holy Bible, New International Version®, NIV®. Copyright © 1973, 1978, 1984, 2011 by Biblica, Inc.™ Used by permission of Zondervan. All rights reserved. www.zondervan.com The "NIV" and "New International Version" are trademarks registered in the United States Patent and Trademark Office by Biblica, Inc.™

VERSION NUMBER 12/11/24

To Katie,

For your enduring love, unwavering support, and endless supply of laughs and patience. You teach me daily what it means to live and love well. And here's hoping for the day when Buffalo Wild Wings will realize that their $0.25 wing night can sometimes help soulmates meet.

To Olivia and Sam,

You two are the greatest things I've ever had a part in during this life. Thank you for the grace and patience you offer me as I try to be the best dad possible—and remembering that really means learning to just trust you both and be myself as I love and support you in every way possible. You two make every day a blessing and an adventure.

Nobody escapes being wounded. We are all wounded people, whether physically, emotionally, mentally, or spiritually. The main question is not, "How can we hide our wounds?" so we don't have to be embarrassed, but "How can we put our woundedness in the service of others?" When our wounds cease to be a source of shame, and become a source of healing, we have become wounded healers.

—Henri Nouwen

The truth is that falling hurts. The dare is to keep being brave and feel your way back up.

—Brené Brown, *Rising Strong*

Contents

Foreword by Jorge Acevedo | ix
Preface | xiii
Acknowledgments | xv
Introduction | xvii

Chapter 1: Accepting Our Powerlessness | 1
Chapter 2: Accepting Our Right Size and God's Too | 12
Chapter 3: Accepting Ourselves, Good, Bad, and Otherwise | 21
Chapter 4: Accepting and Giving Forgiveness | 33
Chapter 5: Accepting Our Families of Origin | 42
Chapter 6: Accepting Our Role as Healthy Parents | 53
Chapter 7: Accepting Our Vocations Without Giving Up Our Lives | 62
Chapter 8: Accepting Our Ongoing Soul Work | 72
Chapter 9: Accepting a Life of Service to God, Neighbor, and Self | 82
A Final Word—For Now | 88

Bibliography | 91

Foreword

THERE IS A HUGE difference between knowledge and wisdom. Think about it this way. Knowledge is the accumulation of understanding and is vitally important. For example, I want my mechanic to have knowledge about my car's inner workings. If he or she is working on my brakes, knowledge of brake pads, calipers and brake fluid is essential, especially after I get it out of the shop and try to stop my car at the traffic light.

But you can have all kinds of knowledge garnered through study, training and research and not be wise. In my sixty-four-plus years of life but especially in my forty years as a pastor, I have watched some of the most knowledgeable people in the world around things like business, sports, and even church life act very foolishly and make really unhealthy, unwise decisions. Simple knowledge does not make a person wise.

So, what makes a person wise? The Bible, especially in the book of Proverbs, points to "the fear of the Lord" as the starting place of wisdom. In Prov 9:10 (NIV), Solomon, considered the wisest man of his time, wrote, "The fear of the LORD is the beginning of wisdom, and knowledge of the Holy One is understanding." Wisdom, according to Solomon, finds its starting place in an awe-filled, respectful relationship with the one who is the author of all of life, God.

In this book, *Grace Rediscovered*, Ben Gosden offers wisdom that finds its moorings in God too. It's not just knowledge. And that is because Ben is a serious apprentice of Jesus. Here's how I know this. I am a pastor and as an "insider" to professional ministry, I know all our "dirty little secrets." It is very easy to allow the work of ministry to become a veneer of professional religious duties. Church life can foster a kind of unhealthy inauthenticity. "Never let 'em see you sweat" can become your unspoken mantra as you "handle the sacred things." Now, please hear me, I'm not blaming the church. We do this to ourselves for the most part. But in this book, Ben tells his truth of sinking into a place of utter desperation and by the grace and mercy of God finding his way out of his addiction to alcohol. This makes Ben a reliable and wise companion on the road to healing.

In these pages, he wisely shares with us the people, places, and processes that any person can use to recover and heal from their everyday addictions, afflictions and compulsive behaviors. For women and men to find deliverance from these requires other people, a community of fellow sojourners who "have been there and done that" on a recovery issue and are finding ongoing healing in their lives together. The healing Ben writes about also points to safe places where men and women can tell the truth about their real struggles with "hurts, habits, and hang-ups." These can be in the rooms of traditional or Christian recovery, a therapist's office, a retreat with a spiritual director, or at a coffee shop with a sponsor. Ben especially outlines a healthy and holy process that finds its roots both in the Bible and the twelve steps of Alcoholics Anonymous. We all need handles to grasp as we make our journey out of the pits into which we fall.

Ben's wisdom is grounded in his lived experience as a grateful follower of Jesus who is experiencing daily recovery from alcohol addiction. Let this book serve as a pathway to the peace that God wants to give you. God the Father calls you his "beloved." God the Son gave his life and rose from the dead on your behalf. And God the Holy Spirit lives to empower you not only to overcome your addictions, afflictions, and compulsive behaviors but also gives you the capacity to bless our sin-sick, war-torn, blood-stained planet. It is wise to—like Ben—follow our mysterious triune God on the road to recovery.

Rev. Dr. Jorge Acevedo
Leadership Coach, Writer, Speaker, Retired Pastor

Preface

THIS BOOK IS THE result of a journey—a journey I never imagined I'd take, but one that has shaped my life in ways I can only call miraculous. It's a story of rediscovering grace, not in some far-off, distant place, but in the everyday moments of healing and surrender.

When I first encountered the principles of recovery, I wasn't sure if they were for me. I was struggling with addiction in the traditional sense, but I was also searching for something more—for freedom, for healing, for a deeper sense of self. What I found was that the path to healing isn't about perfection, but about progress, about learning to trust in a Power greater than ourselves, and about allowing grace to transform us.

As I walked this road, I began to realize that the principles of recovery are not just for those dealing with addiction; they are for all of us. We all carry wounds, and we all need healing. In this book, I've shared my own experiences and the lessons I've learned in the hope that they might encourage you to discover the grace that's available to you as well.

Grace Rediscovered isn't just a book about recovery; it's a book about living a life rooted in grace, healing, and hope. Whether you're familiar with the twelve steps or completely new to the concept, the journey of recovery can offer something valuable to anyone who is seeking more peace, more freedom, and more connection in their life.

PREFACE

Thank you for walking this journey with me. I hope that through these pages you, too, will rediscover the power of grace in your own life.

Acknowledgments

To my friends in recovery, thank you for sharing your wisdom, your struggles, and your hope. You have been my teachers, my companions, and my lifeline. I'm forever grateful for the fellowship we share and the lessons I've learned from walking this road with you.

To my spiritual coach and friend Dr. Brian Russell, thank you for guiding me deeper into faith and for showing me what it means to live a life grounded in grace. Your insight, encouragement, and gentle nudges have been invaluable to my spiritual life.

A special thank you to everyone who read drafts of sections of this book, gave much-needed feedback, or gave a kind word when I needed it most. All of you and the support you offered helped shape these pages, and your belief in this message means the world to me.

Lastly, to those who have journeyed through their own recovery and discovered their own path of healing, thank you for inspiring me to share this story. This book is for all of us—trudging the road to happy destiny, finding grace in the everyday, and learning to live with open hearts.

Introduction

SLOWLY BUT SURELY, I came to realize enough was enough. I was increasingly burned out in my job. I was losing patience with the people I loved most. And I was tired—I was so tired—of the routine and the work and the stuff that had brought me to this place of exhaustion. Something had to change.

Maybe you've heard of an existential crisis. It's part of our human condition. It's that moment when you become keenly aware that the inner you and outer you are not in alignment. Sometimes it happens during a normal transitional phase like becoming a parent, or changing jobs, or discovering that you are now an empty nester. Sometimes it happens with the death of a loved one, or in some other moment when you're confronted with the inevitability of death. It's the moment when we come to realize that enough is enough and something has to change.

If you've picked up this book, I'm going to assume it's because you, like me, are familiar with the symptoms of a real, honest, stop-you-in-your-tracks existential crisis. I don't know what brought it on for you—maybe neither do you. That's okay. Chances are, even if you don't know what brought it on, you have begun to recognize the symptoms.

Symptom 1: Fatigue. You begin to notice just how tired you are. Tired of where you are in life. Tired of your routine. Tired of people. Maybe your job just doesn't make sense or bring fulfillment like it once did.

INTRODUCTION

Symptom 2: Confusion. The things that used to make sense make less and less sense. You begin to question the most basic parts of your life. The direction and purpose you once had seems fleeting and you find yourself feeling lost.

Symptom 3: Angst. You may feel a restless, unresolved, energy. Christian theologian Richard Rohr refers to this angst as the nagging question, "What are we really doing when we are doing what we're doing?"[3] I know, it's a horrible question, most of us, me included, would prefer to remain focused on the distractions—decorating a home, pursuing a relationship, advancing a career, chasing our dreams.

And these are just three common symptoms of an existential crisis. If these symptoms seem familiar, you're not alone. I think every adult with half an ounce of self-awareness has a moment like this—when they step back from the doldrums of their everyday and ask some of life's larger questions. In these moments, if we're truly honest with ourselves, we can acknowledge the anxieties and fears we carry deep within us. Maybe they are fears we've carried since childhood. Maybe they are insecurities we picked up during adolescence. Whatever those fears are, and regardless of when they began, we may discover them living just below the surface—masked by our adult identities, hidden beneath the facade of our good work or polished personas.

I am writing this book because I experienced one of these crises. And in spite of the uncomfortable symptoms, and the unwelcome questions, I came to see how my acknowledgement of the misalignment in my life was a kind of threshold. It was in this moment that I discovered a way not to avoid the discomfort but to propel my journey toward greater alignment, healing, and eventually a reality where I felt fully alive.

It all started as I approached my fortieth birthday. Something about the transition into midlife began to make me question myself. I'm actually impressed that I made it almost forty years before this crisis hit me. All of my life I had felt a little different. But I learned to adapt. I worked to fit in so others would accept me. I did all the things that would make people see me as

INTRODUCTION

a good person, a leader, a high achiever. I sought out ways to feel loved and accepted—even if it meant hiding a piece of my true self in order to feel safe. But all the while, the angst inside of me was building. It reached its pinnacle in the fall of 2020, as the world was in the throes of a global pandemic.

Today, I can tell you, "I am an alcoholic." But I didn't know it at the time. All I knew then was that I had begun to feel like my daily habit had become more than a quarantine recreation. I couldn't verbalize fully what I was feeling about that either, but I knew two things had happened—I had become more and more uncomfortable with my routine, and I couldn't easily break the daily habit. I had stopped drinking alcohol earlier in 2020—for a whole one hundred days. And then, like many bad habits, COVID-19 and the fear of the world ending sent me right back onto the routine without a way out. By day I was a functional pastor of a growing church, a faithful husband and father, and an upstanding member of society—a successful leader in most anyone's eyes. But by night I would sink into a quiet abyss fueled by alcohol. I felt comforted by the awareness that I wasn't outwardly destructive. I was just seeking an inward escape. I knew a stiff drink could unwind the tightness in my neck faster than any stretch. I didn't know then what I know now. I wasn't comfortable in my own skin—I've never been comfortable in my own skin. The tightness in my neck was the result of my constant striving to be perfect in all things for all people at all times. I was afraid I wouldn't be loved if I didn't succeed. And I was terribly afraid someone would eventually sniff me out as the imposter I felt like I was in life. So alcohol did for me what I could not do for myself—it helped me tolerate the angst of being me.

It took nearly two years of sitting with the symptoms of a misaligned life, but finally in January of 2022 I was able to recognize my desire to live a sober life. It's hard to describe why it's so difficult to face the truth that a simple daily recreation has gotten out of hand. It took another four months before I realized that I was an alcoholic. Up until then, sobriety (like everything else in my life) was simply another goal. Something to aspire to, work toward, and achieve. I thought I could conquer this like I conquered everything else in life—with my wits and self-will. Facing my alcoholism, meant I had to give up the biggest myth of all in life, which was the myth of thinking I could run my own life by my own strength.

I vividly recall the day this myth finally shattered into a thousand pieces. No, there were no bright lights. Instead, it came over me like a sinking feeling of despair one sunny afternoon. There was no voice from heaven. Instead, it was only my own internal voice that led me to these words: "I don't think it's normal to worry this much about drinking." This slow and silent reality shook me to my core. After that, I found a sponsor.

My sponsor, a friend who had been sober for many years, gently led me to the truth all human beings must either reckon with or choose to ignore at their own peril—we are all spiritually sick and only God can save us. I entered the rooms of recovery thinking I needed a quick fix for my lasting despair. But, like so many before me, I began to realize my drinking was only an outward sign of a spiritual sickness I had never been able to acknowledge. All of the nights when I wondered if I would snap before I could relax with a drink, all of the worry I carried everyday about what people thought of me—it was all part of a deeper and more spiritual malady. And it turns out I wasn't as weird as I thought after all. Maybe you, unlike me, are not an alcoholic. That's good news. But it doesn't prevent you from feeling the deeper unrest and crisis that so many of us feel when we discover that we really are finite, limited, often lonely, and so often misaligned in our daily routine.

For me, my existential crisis is lived out in my recovery from the disease of alcoholism. I wake up each day remembering my alcoholism is a disease whose symptoms are an outward expression of an inward struggle for peace and hope—a peace and hope that comes when I rely less on my false self, but instead learn to love my true self more.

What is it for you? Can you name the source of your misalignment, your angst, or your discomfort? What is leading you to ask bigger questions of your life? Whatever brought you here, to

INTRODUCTION

this place in your journey, you are right on time. You couldn't have rushed yourself here before you were ready. And now that you're here, you're not shutting down or holding back.

So, if you're ready, I want to be a field guide as you go on this journey. I won't have answers for all your questions. But I do have my own story to share. I can promise that you are not alone in your struggle. And I can point out a few lessons I've learned that just might help you see your life—the good, the bad, and the sometimes ugly—as a gift. The journey is grace because it leads us back to the God who loves us most. It's the cross Jesus invites us to carry because it leads us to a promise of new life—a life our existential crises lead us to long for. So welcome, fellow sojourner, and let's get started!

BG
Ordinary Time
2024

Chapter 1: Accepting Our Powerlessness

> *But he said to me, "My grace is sufficient for you, for power is made perfect in weakness." So I will boast all the more gladly of my weaknesses, so that the power of Christ may dwell in me.*
>
> —2 CORINTHIANS 12:9

The Myth of Power

WHEN YOU'RE A CHILD, adults seem all-powerful. They do what they want, when they want. It's a freedom children long for. Education and job training become important goals because we're told they will get us where we want to go—they unlock the power adults enjoy. The goals of freedom and autonomy guide us toward our ultimate aim in life—the one we don't always dare to name aloud—power.

When I was a kid, I couldn't wait to grow up. The adults around me were larger than life. They had jobs, money, and the ability to make decisions that shaped the future of everyone around them. At the time, I had no idea what a myth it all was. Kids don't typically see the pain adults carry or the stress that weighs them down. Life is full of failings and stumbles as we grow and mature. And adults work really hard to hide their weariness.

Now that I'm an adult, I've realized that kids aren't the only ones who buy into the myth of power. Most adults seem to believe it about themselves, too. Few know how to talk about the failings and stumbles that come with aging and maturing. It's easier to maintain the illusion of having everything together. Adults might be weary, but one day we believe we can attain the power to end our weariness and sufficiently conquer our world.

The first step to learning the truth about life is unlearning the lessons adults taught us. This unlearning requires us to question the teachings of those important adults in our lives—whether these lessons were imparted directly or indirectly. Even as we question, we have to muster a certain amount of grace. The real lesson is realizing that they (and we) were doing the best they could with the light they had at the time. They were learning to be human and to navigate life in human ways, which is often messy and imperfect. And that takes a lot of grace.

The pursuit of power is a prime example of a lesson that informs how we live as human beings. Unlearning this lesson means rethinking the ways we've lived and pursued our own goals. For example, we love modern technology because we believe it gives us power over resources like time and energy. We love earning money because it gives us power over the wants and desires of our hearts. We adopt healthy habits like taking vitamins, working out, and eating well because we believe these practices give us power over the reality of death.

The pursuit of power shows up in less obvious ways, too. We might tell a lie because it gives us power over the fear of being wrong, feeling foolish, or disappointing others. We might cheat a little because it gives us power over the fear of inadequacy or because we believe we deserve something we haven't earned. We engage in unhealthy relationships or practices because they give us power over our most basic carnal desires like being loved or enjoying sexual satisfaction.

The pursuit of power might not always appear to be at the forefront of our thinking, but it's there. It lurks beneath the surface of our being. It fuels our desire to be more, to do more, and to have more. Like a drug, power gives us a dopamine hit when it pays off. That satisfaction we feel is enjoyable and we want more and more of it. Deep down, we also believe that power is the key to conquering our deepest fears. It's scary to imagine a life where we don't feel important. We want meaning and purpose. We want security and certainty. And if those desires aren't met naturally, we will exercise whatever power we can find to meet them.

This all works as part of a power economy that lives below the surface of our lives. We exercise power over others and our ourselves. And we accept (or not) that some people inevitably have power over us. It's a give and take. But the goal is to come out on the positive end of the balance sheet.

The problem is that exercising power works until it doesn't. What happens when life throws us a curveball that proves we never really had much power over our lives at all—when a loved one dies, when tragedy strikes, when things don't work out according to our plans, etc.?

It turns out these are the moments that teach us the hard lesson that we are not as powerful as we think we are. And there's nothing we can do to change that, try as we might.

This book is a book about finding healing and recovery. I know from my own story that the first step toward that healing comes when we finally come to terms with the fact that we aren't nearly as powerful as we wish we were. Once we can name our powerlessness, we can begin to experience God's healing. We cannot experience the healing power of God until we finally accept the fact that we are not god. And it turns out that not being God is perfectly okay.

Powerlessness Is the Key to Freedom

Healing begins with the acknowledgement that we need to be delivered from something. One of the hardest truths of adulthood is that we are limited, finite beings. Contrary to what we've been taught, we cannot conquer the world. We are human—nothing more, nothing less.

Since the dawn of time, humans have tried to prove how exceptional they are. We strive to be the most special, with the most unique skills, standing out as the best there ever was. We invent things. We go to war to conquer or defend things. We build and break down. Our exceptional talents and gifts are what has propelled humans forward in history. And a side benefit has been the satisfaction we enjoy knowing we have extraordinary power compared to other creatures in creation.

Add to it all that our modern social media age helps us broadcast our exceptional abilities even more. We now have platforms for everyone to broadcast their uniqueness as loudly as possible. No one wants to be ordinary. Ordinary people are rarely celebrated. From a young age, we're taught to strive to be extraordinary, to win, and to excel in all things. It's a lot of pressure to put on a kid, so it's no wonder we're seeing anxiety and depression in kids at younger and younger ages. The expectations they face are often impossible to meet. When we fail—and we all do at some point—the weight of those unmet expectations leads to grief and despair.

Much like Jesus was tempted to gain the praise of nations if he only worshiped Satan, we are tempted to seek the kind of relevance that celebrates our unique talents. This drive stems from a deep fear that our lives will be meaningless if, at the end, we don't leave a legacy of power and importance. So we spend our lives trying to hide our limitations from ourselves.

But what if being the human we were made to be, nothing more and nothing less, *is* the most amazing thing we could ever do? Being delivered from our false notions of importance so we can accept the fullness of who we are as human beings is a gift that can change our lives from the inside out.

Being human does come with challenges. Feelings can be hard to manage. Circumstances are quite often beyond our control. We are, whether we want to admit it or not, ultimately powerless over people, places, and things. Admitting this powerlessness, however, can be the beginning of a new life where we finally come to terms with the dis-ease we carry deep inside.

ACCEPTING OUR POWERLESSNESS

Paul gives us a road map toward this transformation: "I do not understand my own actions. For I do not do what I want, but I do the very thing I hate."[1] The disconnect Paul describes is the tension we live with daily. Unless we are entirely unaware of ourselves, we know there are moments when we choose the easy path, cut corners, or even make poor choices out of fear, laziness, or ignorance. Cycles form and we repeat these misguided things over and over again.

I spent over ten years of my adult life as a daily drinker. Now, as a person in long-term recovery, I can tell you that most days I didn't want to drink. I'd wake up feeling terrible, irritable with my family, and doing anything I could to quickly hydrate and shake off the awful feelings. I'd vow not to drink that evening. Surely, I'd learned my lesson, and no evening of booze and television was worth feeling that way again. And yet, like clockwork, 8:00 PM would roll around, and without a second thought, I'd start pouring drinks, escaping to a world confined to the television and free from the stress and discomfort of living in my own skin.

I was powerless, and my life was unmanageable. On the surface, things looked different. I held a good job. I was present for my wife and kids—or at least I did a good job of making it seem that way. I wasn't ruining my life like many others who share their stories in recovery rooms. But I couldn't stop, and the truth of that inability began to eat away at my soul. Surely, I was too smart, too talented to be an alcoholic! Surely, I could find a way to manage this problem I quietly carried around, fearing others might eventually find me out.

The question wasn't whether something was wrong with me. Something was definitely wrong. The real question was whether I could finally admit there was something wrong and that I couldn't fix it myself. Accepting that truth was the threshold to a new way of living I so desperately wanted.

What do you feel powerless over? What patterns are present in your life where you feel out of control or unable to change?

---

1. Rom 7:15.

Maybe it's food, maybe it's working too much, maybe it's gossiping, or maybe it's avoiding hard tasks out of fear and insecurity. It's hard to admit we have a problem. It's hard to admit our lives are unmanageable if we believe we can be the sole captains of our own lives. So instead of accepting that truth, we double down on our efforts to control our lives and the lives of those around us. If only the world would behave the way we think it should, all would be okay. Except the world will never behave according to our will. And we must learn to be okay with that.

A life-changing truth to embrace is that we are not the sum of our efforts. Our value in this world does not come from what we do. The theological term for this misconception is works righteousness. The apostle Paul warned against thinking we are saved by our own doing: "For by grace you have been saved."[2] This is not a product of our own works, but it comes as a gift from God.

People of faith understand this concept. Of course salvation comes from Jesus, we think. Of course we can't create our own salvation. Yet how many of us confess this truth but live as though we can really save ourselves? Our daily lives tell the story of how we worry ourselves to death over things we cannot control. We even spend our time dwelling on the past or worrying about the future—neither of which is a current reality. We think if only we try hard enough, work hard enough, do enough, we can become the people we believe we should be, especially the kind of people others will admire.

Admitting our powerlessness means accepting that we cannot control the things we spend most of our lives trying to control. No amount of work will make us worthy because we will never outrun the hole in our soul by our own efforts. We are saved by grace. This is a God who wants nothing more than for us to calm down and give our worries and need for control over to the God who loved us and formed our inmost being before we did anything to prove our worth. Salvation is on the horizon when we let go and allow God to become our ultimate source of power. That's where true freedom is unlocked.

---

2. Eph 2:8.

The failings and stumbles of life can serve a greater purpose of helping us discover not only who we are but also who God is in the midst of life's most crushing moments. It's hard to fully understand the purpose of these moments while we're in them. The real growth comes from the lessons we learn through our failings. God's grace can be found in the meaning we derive from our shortcomings. Business leaders talk about learning to "fail forward," and there's something to that. But for people of faith dealing with life's most significant challenges, we know that failing forward can also mean falling into something—the very arms of God.

God as Our Source of Power

I'm not in control of all things. God is actually in control. That sounds fair in theory, but it's so hard to accept it as the guiding truth of our lives. There is an inner barrier that keeps us from believing that we are not in control. It's called ego.

Ego is the protective barrier we form at an early age. It's the outer coating of our soul—the layer of armor we hold to protect our fragile selves from the pain of life. Ego is what keeps us from fully embracing the power of God in our lives. In terms of faith, ego is the impulse to whittle the gospel down to a single moral issue or set of moral issues. It's the inclination to divide everyone into "us versus them." It's the powerful force that fools us into thinking being right is our ultimate aim in life. Ego is our lifeline to feeling like we can be in control of all things.

This grand ego must be let go if we are to experience transformation and healing. Otherwise we will simply try to engineer our own salvation according to our terms and methods built on our power and control. It's hard to give up the pilot's seat when it comes to navigating our own lives. Try as we might we spend so much energy trying to engineer our lives and our future only to realize along the way that we can't force life to unfold according to the way we wish it would. Ego would tell us to just try harder and it might work out. But the reality is we will end up disappointed and exhausted if we spend our lives trying to force things to happened according to our will. Our ego makes us feel powerful but it quietly drains us of our emotional energy.

I felt this tension in the ways I pastored my churches. I wanted so badly to lead churches to grow. Of course I didn't admit this longing openly. I had enough self-awareness to know you don't confess those sorts of things in polite company. But everything I said and did said being successful was my ultimate goal. All things had to lead to church growth. I agonized over attendance and our budget. I found myself sorely hurt if anyone left our church. And, worst of all, I carried the stress of it all home at night where I would drink to relieve the pressure valve so I could rise the following day to chart our course a little more.

After two years of the COVID-19 pandemic, unending church life, and completing my doctor of ministry degree, the pain of trying to control everything so tightly began to set in. I began to feel weary. I lacked creativity. And a low boiling depression began to bubble up in my soul. My ego had led me to a fork in the road where I had to choose whether I wanted to continue down a path of feeding my ego's insatiable appetite for success or choose a slower path. Luckily, I had a few people in my life who strongly advised me to take some time off.

When I decided to take a month off from church work, I had grand plans of growing, exploring, and having the greatest sabbatical anyone had ever attempted. But God had other plans. I had begun my sobriety journey as a social experiment earlier in the year. By the time my sabbatical began those plans had slowly fallen through leaving me with just a simple plan for my time off—spend time with God, spend time with my family, spend time in my recovery, and spend time tending my own soul.

What began as a sabbatical reward for my hard work and success quietly became a self-imposed rehab stint. My ego had taken me as far as I could go with it. I saw the destination of where I was heading if I continued the path of letting my ego be in charge and it wasn't pretty. I needed a new source of power because I saw the rock bottom I was spiraling toward. It wasn't a dramatic crash like you imagine from an addict in a movie scene. Instead it was a slow and direct crash fueled by my substance addiction and my desire to be loved and admired by others. I realized that I could do it all on my own until one day I couldn't do it anymore. Eventually I would finally let my family down, burn out for good in my vocation, and become another statistic of how alcoholism is a progressive and deadly disease.

I have been a Christian for my entire life. I was baptized in the church as a baby and confirmed as an adolescent. I'm seminary trained and I have preached about God's power and salvation on a weekly basis for close to fifteen years. But it was in coming to terms with my own recovery from alcoholism that I finally learned how to begin to accept this power in my own life.

Addiction is just an outward sign of an inward disease. And the disease I was experiencing is no different than the disease we all carry. We want to be all-powerful and control our lives. We don't want to be vulnerable or weak. We want to protect ourselves at all costs and live a comfortable life. We're taught that when life gives you lemons, make lemonade. The hard truth of life and the power we think we have is that when life gives us lemons, we just need to give those lemons to God and trust God to do what is needed with them. It's not solely our job to make everything right. This requires acceptance and a rigorous honesty about our own limitations. We can't grow until we accept the truth about our powerlessness.

Starting the Path Toward Freedom

Acceptance comes with God's help. Richard Rohr cites the work of Gregory of Nyssa when he says, "Sin happens whenever we refuse to keep growing."[3] I think that's true. Growth requires an intentionality of focus that is easy to lose and hard to regain when we get too locked into life's routines. At that point it's much easier to let our thoughts and opinions become fixed. But fixed mindsets breed things like fear, hatred, or indifference. We don't mean for

---

3. Rohr, *Falling Upward*, 74.

this to happen. But the absence of a growth mindset eventually means we become rigid in our thinking.

As kids, we think adults have all the answers to life's questions. Little do we know they are just doing the best they can with the light they have. When we age into adulthood, we learn that the journey all adults must take is the journey of learning how to embrace not knowing as the path toward true growth. Along the way we learn how to stop fighting against it and accept the reality of our powerlessness. We grow when we let go of the idea that we've got it all figured out.

Or, as Paul reminds us, we are learning how to "put an end to childish ways" to embrace our true adulthood, which is maturity in Christ.[4] Ironically, children can teach us a lot about this growth mindset. Children know what it means to depend on a power greater than themselves. They love the art of learning and the excitement of embracing life as it comes. Children don't tend to spend lots of time and energy trying to orchestrate their lives. Instead, they demonstrate an openness to each day as it comes.

Adults could learn a lot from a child's openness by embracing a growth mindset. Growth mindset refuses to believe we have all the answers. It sees the world with an insatiable sense of curiosity and realizes that being judgmental is a protective shield that surrounds the insecurity we all carry when certainty cannot be promised. A growth mindset is a daily invitation into the mystery of God's will unfolding in our lives. It's an invitation to let go of our need to control all things. But it's not a refusal to take accountability for what we can do. God's grace is offered freely, but we have a response to make in accepting that grace in our lives. Like children who learn new lessons every day, we can learn the power of grace, our need for it, and our role in accepting it as God's offers it as we learn to trust God as the ultimate source of power in our lives.

I think Christian culture loses its way when its only focus is on stances on whatever the issue of the day might be. It's easy to be loud and boisterous about the things we think we know. But our faith is lived out in real life and in real time and that

---

4. 1 Cor 13:11.

requires accepting that life is, at its core, a mystery unfolding each day. This means most things in our life are rarely black and white. They are beautiful, complicated, and experienced in living color. A life that welcomes growth also welcomes a constant bent toward learning. And this requires an acceptance that we rarely actually have all of the answers.

We can respond to God's love and leading with an open mind. We can seek to embrace mystery and give ourselves over to a power that is truly greater than ourselves. This way of responding recognizes that while we cannot be the primary driver of our lives, we can ride shotgun while we allow God to be the driver. We can keep an eye on the navigation system, ask lots of questions, and even come to love the experience of the ride itself as we give God the wheel and know our proper role.

And accepting the truth of taking on a growth mindset becomes the beginning of discovering our own path toward healing—one marked by growing in a new understanding of who is in charge, how much power we really don't possess, and how much we need God's help daily.

This journey of growth and healing takes its next steps in discovering our need to rightsize ourselves considering our lack of control and need for God's help and healing. Being rightsized is not meant to diminish ourselves so much as to discover who we truly are.

Chapter 2: Accepting Our Right Size and God's Too

Every one of us is shadowed by an illusory person: a false self. This is the man I want myself to be but who cannot exist, because God does not know anything about him. And to be unknown of God is altogether too much privacy. My false and private self is the one who wants to exist outside the reach of God's will and God's love—outside of reality and outside of life.[1]

—THOMAS MERTON

Settling Into Our True Size

SELF-PRESERVATION IS OUR NATURAL goal in life. We want to protect ourselves at all costs. At some point growing up, we transition from expressing our feelings and needs freely as children to guarding those feelings more closely. We become self-conscious as we mature into adolescence and adulthood, with that comes a strong worry about what others think of us. We eventually learn safety means trying to control as much of life as we can. Whether we realize it or not, the art of control is a protective measure we take to keep ourselves safe.

---

1. Merton, *New Seeds of Contemplation*, 34.

ACCEPTING OUR RIGHT SIZE AND GOD'S TOO

Being vulnerable is the antithesis of self-preservation because it requires that we dare to be authentic and not hide from the world out of fear. Brené Brown writes about the risk of vulnerability. She notes her own struggle to embrace vulnerability as a limiting factor of experiencing the true fullness of life, including the joy of love and belonging.[2] Vulnerability is risky, so we become selective and measured about how we express our feelings and how we express ourselves to the world. Instead of expressing our feelings like small children, we create a protective outer layer for others. That outer layer has an imaginary doorman who decides who, if anyone, is allowed in to see the real you. As a result, we play it safe but experience life on limited terms.

For me, this routine of self-preservation began to fall apart when I realized that I drank daily and, try as I might, I couldn't stop. It turned out I did not have the control I wanted over my own habits. I would wake up every morning with a headache and hangover pledging I wouldn't do that again. And then, almost without thinking, I would find myself some twelve hours later pouring a drink and beginning the vicious cycle all over again. It was the big secret I kept from everyone, including those closest to me.

I couldn't imagine having the vulnerability to tell someone, anyone, that I had a problem. I would make up excuses, especially to my wife, to downplay the problem I knew was lurking underneath the surface. I didn't tell the truth. Or I at least stretched the truth to not sound as bad as it was. As long as I could pull myself together after, my dirty little secret was safe with me.

It seems insane, especially if you're not someone who has struggled with the disease of addiction. But I promise there's reason and logic hidden in the insanity. Drinking was the outward symptom of an inward problem. I didn't know what to do with the stress I felt. I didn't know how to process my feelings. I didn't know what to do with the deep fear I felt when people criticized me, when I felt left out, or when I thought I might fail. I had no idea about the effects of my childhood trauma—of growing up where my parents constantly screamed, where safety and peace

2. Brown, *Daring Greatly*, 2.

were hard to come by, and where emotional distance was often the only thing keeping any peace at all. It was too much to bear, so I numbed it out instead.

All of this weighed on me in extraordinarily heavy yet quiet ways. I didn't know how to talk about any of it. And I was too afraid to tell anyone about it. I escaped instead. I could self-medicate through drinking and essentially escape those feelings that quietly built up and swirled around in my soul. It was sort of like finding an elevator hatch where I could pour a stiff drink (or three), push the button, and escape the discomfort for the rest of the evening.

I had to come to terms with the fact that this cycle was my way of controlling life whenever I felt uncomfortable. By day I would exhaust myself by trying to control everything in my life. By night I would escape to relieve the pressure. Rinse and repeat.

Are you tired of trying to hold everything together in your life? Are you struggling with the weight of it all? Do you have an inner angst that feels like it might eventually swallow you up? It's so hard. And the harsh reality is that people really won't always do what you want them to do. You can't fix everything. People can be assholes for no good reason. Bad things happen to good people. And we often don't get answers for any of this on the terms we want.

It might not be drinking or substances for you. But I'm willing to bet you have a way of medicating yourself when discomfort arises. Maybe you work more hours and give yourself to your job more than anything or anyone else. You might eat in the hope that you can eventually satiate the discomfort. Maybe you escape into porn or other sexual escapades pretending those feelings won't eventually come back. Or you might be the person who's addicted to digging in and trying harder and harder to control anything and everything around you. Somehow, someway you find a way to escape the discomfort.

A big piece of embracing our powerlessness is coming to terms with our need to be rightsized. *Merriam-Webster* defines "rightsize" as "to undergo a reduction to an optimal size."[3] I believe most of us

---

3. *Merriam-Webster*, "Rightsize."

need some sort of transformation to find our optimal size in life whether it's becoming smaller or bigger to fit who God made us to be To think you might be able to control everything around you is to exercise power you simply do not have. And expecting that you can change that truth means you have a perspective that is much too out of whack for your human existence.

A friend in recovery told me about a time when he was being particularly controlling. He shared in a recovery meeting about what was going on and his frustration that the situation wouldn't bend to his will and just turn out the way he knew was best for everyone.

After the meeting an old guy said to him, "What's the difference between you and God?" My friend thought that was a ridiculous question, but he was game to know what the old man would say so he asked what was the difference. The man said, "God doesn't go around pretending to be you."

Emotional and spiritual health begins with coming to terms with our need to rightsize our perspective in life. And this means acknowledging that God is God, and we are not. We are not as big as we project ourselves to be. And we're not nearly as small as we're afraid we might be. We are who we are. We're just not God-sized. And that's a good thing.

Our wants and wishes are not the most important thing in the world. Our views and opinions do not reign supreme. People are not idiots or mean if they do not respond to our every beck and call. Contrary to how we might act on any given day, we are not the center of the universe. We cannot play God. And trying to control everything as though we are God will make us incredibly miserable.

Giving Our Lives to God

So if we can't play God, then how do we relate to God in a healthier way? How do we find the right size for ourselves, not too big and not too small?

Christians have a cultural milestone known across the various traditions. It could be called something different depending on the church or denomination you're in, but it's there. I'm a Southerner born in the heart of the Bible Belt, so we call it "giving our lives to Jesus." This surrendering is often viewed as the beginning of the life of faith. To give ourselves—heart, mind, and soul—to God is to surrender ourselves to the One who made us and who we believe will ultimately care for us more than we could care for ourselves alone. This is the nature of God's love. It's what Jesus means when he uplifts the law of loving God with all our heart, mind, soul, and strength as being one half of the greatest commandment.[4] When we give ourselves fully to God, we demonstrate our love and trust in the God who first reaches out to love us.

Scripture tells us, "For God so loved the world that he gave his only Son, so that everyone who believes in him may not perish but may have eternal life."[5] However to "believe in" is more than intellectual agreement. The Greek word for believe is *pisteuó* which means to put our whole trust and confidence in.[6] In other words, when we believe in Jesus we stake our life on the promise that he will care for us in this life and beyond.

Kierkegaard writes about how Jesus wants followers, not admirers.

> What then, is the difference between an admirer and a follower? A follower is or strives to be what he admires. An admirer, however, keeps himself personally detached. He fails to see that what is admired involves a claim upon him, and thus he fails to be or strive to be what he admires.[7]

So it's important to note that this life of loving God is a lifetime of relationship. And it's a lifetime built one day at a time. As much as Christians want to claim things like Christian worldviews

---

4. Matt 22:37.
5. John 3:16.
6. Sentell, "John 3:16."
7. Kierkegaard, *Practice in Christianity*, 233.

or Christian values, we fail to go as far as the Bible calls us to go—to surrender our lives daily to the way of Jesus.

This loving surrender is so much bigger than a one-time occurrence in our life. It's not just a private prayer we pray in our heart during an emotional worship service as a teenager. It's not just an altar call we answer out of a deep sense of guilt. It's not something we passively observe as we sit through confirmation or membership classes. It's a daily surrender of our will to God as we seek to put our whole trust in God's loving grace in our lives.

If chapter 1 of this book describes the ways we seek to control every aspect of our lives, then chapter 2, and the rightsizing of ourselves before God, seeks to show that we all need find a willingness to truly believe in a Power greater than ourselves. Surrendering our lives to the love and care of God is a daily happening if it is to truly be real in our lives.

Surrendering to the power of God's love and care is not easy. It requires us to ruthlessly face our brokenness and become willing to let God repair us from the inside out.[8] It's the transformation of our faith lives from merely agreeing with Jesus to seeking to live according to his will and follow his ways. And if we truly want to live following his way, we must daily give up wanting to follow our own way in life or the way someone told us we should be.

Dietrich Bonhoeffer said, "When Christ calls a man, he bids him come and die."[9] The journey of maturity is learning that the self Christ bids to come and die is the false self we create. It's the self we make to make ourselves feel safe or powerful or important. It's the self we wrench ourselves into being for the sake of other people's approval. It's the self someone told us we should be so they would love us. It's the self we carefully construct to fit in even if it means making ourselves too big or too small in the process.

When that false self is offered to Christ in full surrender, we are slowly and surely returned to our true selves. The death of the false self, or the ego, is what makes way for the true self to be

---

8. *Alcoholics Anonymous*, 13.
9. Bonhoeffer, *Cost of Discipleship*, 44.

known—the self that is uniquely holy and made in the image of God for the sake of love.

Hope and healing come when we surrender our lives and especially our egos to God daily. This surrender requires courage on our part. And the best news of all is that it also requires some amazing grace from God that is readily available to us whenever we are ready to accept it.

Accepting Our Right Size Daily

I love Flannery O'Connor's story *A Good Man is Hard to Find*. It's a classic Southern Gothic tale full of big characters and a grotesque plot twist at the end. The grandmother in the story, much like all matriarchs in O'Connor's stories, is a wretched woman. She's overbearing, judgmental, self-righteous, and terrible to anyone who doesn't agree with the way she sees life. As the family goes on their road trip, you almost want to push her out of the car she's so awful.

There's a scene at the very end of the story (spoiler alert) where The Misfit is holding the grandmother at gun point. As this is happening, the grandmother begins to have a revelation about The Misfit. She sees him for all his hurt and pain. She sees all the ways he has longed for belonging and been left out. She sees his humanity when her own humanity is truly at stake. She tells him he's "one of her babies." It's really a moving and surprising turn of character for this otherwise wretched woman.

Only that's when The Misfit shoots her.

The haunting line O'Connor puts in the mouth of The Misfit says, "She would of been a good woman . . . if it had been somebody there to shoot her every minute of her life."[10]

There is something profound about knowing the brokenness that lives within us. Truly having the knowledge of our own humanity—good, bad, and ugly—is a heavy task to take on, but it's the only path we have toward true freedom. We spend so much of our lives hiding, pretending, trying to be all the things for all

---

10. O'Connor, *Good Man Is Hard to Find*, 151.

ACCEPTING OUR RIGHT SIZE AND GOD'S TOO

the people, and terribly afraid someone might actually find us out for what we are—broken and flawed people desperately afraid we won't know love or meaning or purpose in our life.

Maybe you're a survivor of childhood trauma and abuse. Maybe you lost someone close to you at a young age and it had a profound effect on you. Maybe you've spent your life trying to matter to someone who should have loved you better. All these things that happen to us and the ways they affect us moving forward shape us for better or worse. They become burdens we carry, and their effects compound the pain we feel until we name it all for what it is.

However, having the knowledge of these difficult things—truly naming them and owning the discomfort of our inner pain—can actually turn out to be a gift from God. God meets us in our pain, promising to never leave us. We don't have to merit it. God's presence comes as a promise and a gift. The pain and brokenness, with God's help, can become the thing that leads us back to ourselves.

One of the hardest lessons in life is learning that we can't heal what we don't feel. So we begin the healing by feeling the weight of our brokenness. It's not hard knowing it's there—we know it's there because we work so hard to hide it. It's God's grace that lets us look that brokenness in the face, name it, and begin to feel it wholly.

The sense of competition or jealousy we feel in the workplace is rooted in fear. We're afraid of not being enough—not important or successful or powerful enough. Maybe we were made to feel this way by someone as a kid. Maybe we had a parent or loved one who projected their own insecurity onto us by treating us as less than. We got attention if we were successful at something, so it became part of a Pavlovian response on our part as we grew up—to succeed is to get noticed, and to get noticed is to be loved.

Our fear of abandonment may have been caused by a parent or significant other who left us. We know it wasn't our fault, but deep down we still wonder if there was something, anything, that could have convinced them to stay. Without realizing it we spend the rest of our lives wrenching ourselves into whatever version of ourselves we think will convince someone to stay.

Codependency is defined as "a dysfunctional relationship dynamic where one person assumes the role of 'the giver,' sacrificing their own needs and well-being for the sake of the other, 'the taker.'"[11] It's so easy to fall into patterns of codependency when we want to be loved and accepted. It becomes a tool to have those needs met.

So the pattern is set before we realize it. Be whoever we need to be so we aren't left abandoned, even if it means becoming a false version of ourselves—to have someone not leave is to be loved, even if it costs us our deepest sense of self. If the relationship stays intact (however lopsided or dysfunctional as it may be), then we are safe.

Feeling these hard things means learning to simply sit with the stuff we feel makes us human and fallible and in need of God. It's sort of the opposite of the Americanized version of salvation. There is no pulling ourselves up by our own bootstraps. There is no rubbing dirt in it and moving on. There is no silence that can render our brokenness null and void. It's there, maybe hidden and locked away inside, but it's there.

Healing follows when we name the hard stuff. Carl Jung said, "Until we make the unconscious conscious, it will direct your life and you will call it fate."[12] The path to healing starts by naming the unspoken things in our souls that weigh us down. It comes when we learn to accept it—good, bad and ugly—when we learn to finally turn it all over to God because it's just too much for us to carry on our own. It's costly, but it's healing that will literally save us.

---

11. Psychology Today, "Codependency."
12. Jung, *Aion*, 24–25.

Chapter 3: Accepting Ourselves, Good, Bad, and Otherwise

Owning our story and loving ourselves through that process is the bravest thing that we will ever do.[1]

—BRENÉ BROWN

Being Uncomfortable in Our Own Skin

SELF-ACCEPTANCE CAN FEEL LIKE a superhuman feat. Picture the version of yourself you see first thing in the morning—half-awake, stumbling into the bathroom, when you catch a glimpse in the mirror. What do you notice? Too many wrinkles? A few unwanted rolls? A beautiful person? Or perhaps a mix of the good and not-so-good?

Now think about the "you" that shows up in group settings. Do you feel comfortable and at ease, or are you a bundle of nerves, worrying about what everyone must be thinking? Are you conscious of when you laugh or share an opinion? Do you notice the responses of others and fret if they seem even slightly off? Or do you feel fearless and connected, inside and out?

For me, the feelings of unease began in childhood. I remember, even at a very young age, a nagging sensation in my gut that would arise whenever I found myself in a room full of strangers or

---

1. Brown, *Gifts of Imperfection*, 60.

in a new environment. I didn't know what it was, only that it made me feel sick. I worried about fitting in and being liked.

Growing up, I was the kid on the outskirts—social enough to have friends but just introverted enough to avoid the spotlight. I longed to be liked and accepted. In my mind, being accepted meant I was enough, that I mattered, that I had significance. Anything less felt like a fate worse than death for a self-conscious kid like me; it confirmed the deep loneliness I felt whenever I was alone.

At some point I discovered humor as a way to navigate social situations. I've always enjoyed comedy and had a knack for making people laugh. It became my secret weapon: if I could make you laugh, you wouldn't laugh at me. My middle school teachers didn't always appreciate me using this "superpower" in class, but impressing them wasn't my priority—I wanted to impress my peers. By the time I was a senior in high school, I was voted "Most Friendly," largely because I knew how to be nice and win people over with humor.

When I got to college, I stumbled upon a new tool to unlock the feeling of ease I'd been searching for: alcohol. I still remember my first drink at a bar. My friends cheered me on; I had been a long-time holdout, determined to uphold the "good Christian boy" image I thought I should maintain. The warmth of that liquid as it went down and the sense of ease that rose up almost immediately—suddenly, I felt loose and comfortable in my own skin. I had spent my life searching for that feeling, and there it was. A few beers seemed to solve the mystery.

Of course, my brain did some quick math: if one beer brought me a certain level of ease, then more beers should bring even more comfort. I spent the better part of twenty years trying to prove that hypothesis. But the more I drank, the more I realized that alcohol could only offer a temporary reprieve. Eventually, the anxieties, fears, and worries would creep back in. On the bright side, I wasn't a mean or angry drunk; the more I drank, the funnier I became. It was like having a double superpower—humor and alcohol combined.

No matter what measures I took to numb and escape, the path always led me back to the same place as the day before—I was terribly uncomfortable in my own skin. Sure, alcohol offered momentary relief, a brief reprieve from the weight of constant worry. But the burden always returned the next day, often accompanied by regret over things I may have said, texted, or forgotten during conversations the night before.

Are you tired of carrying that burden in your life? Is the self-consciousness and self-criticism becoming too heavy to bear? Do you find yourself seeking escape through various outlets—food, substances, work, controlling others, pornography, or something else?

With the grace and mercy of God, we have the power to take the first steps toward healing. We must begin by naming the burdens we carry within us. Whether they manifest as childhood trauma, fear, or even a seemingly ordinary case of debilitating self-consciousness, we need to acknowledge them to fully let go and surrender them to God.

Naming the Ugly Stuff

Alcoholism—or "alcohol use disorder"—is a disease that affects 7 percent of the global population fifteen years and older[2] (of course I believe these numbers are low because alcoholism is largely a self-diagnosed disease). However, the experience of being uncomfortable in one's own skin is a far more widespread and prevalent condition, impacting the human experience on a much larger scale.

Do you ever feel like you just don't fit in? Maybe you experience loneliness even when surrounded by a group of people. Perhaps you get lost in your head as your thoughts run wild with feelings of not measuring up, imagining that others look down on you, or believing you're a failure if you don't meet every expectation.

---

2. World Health Organization, *Global Status Report on Alcohol*, xii.

You might be carrying a hurt or trauma so deep that it eats away at you during the quiet moments of life. To cope, you distract yourself—whether through work, food, alcohol, sex, or anything else that provides a brief escape from the pain, even if just for a few fleeting moments.

In Luke 4, Jesus confronts the temptations of being relevant, being spectacular, and being powerful. This passage provides one of the clearest glimpses into the humanity of Jesus, as he encounters struggles familiar to us all. The temptations present a way to escape his current circumstances, offering more comfortable paths that avoid the pain. Instead of facing the difficulties head-on, Satan tempts Jesus with shortcuts that appeal to our deepest desires.

The temptation to be relevant reveals our profound need to be accepted. Satan tempts Jesus by offering power and dominion over all the kingdoms of the world, with one condition: he must bow and worship him. The allure of being revered by the masses could have been strong; after all, to be admired is to feel loved, and to be loved is to feel accepted. But what cost are we willing to pay to satisfy this human longing?

Jesus shows us that worshiping God alone puts us in our proper place—acknowledging God's grace freely and preemptively offered to us. This involves "rightsizing" ourselves, understanding our worth not as arrogance but as a true view of who we are and who we are not. We were created to worship God, and our value is found in living in response to that divine love.

The temptation to be spectacular reflects our desire for our lives to have meaning. Satan challenges Jesus to throw himself from a tall tower, promising that God will save him. The underlying test is to prove his life is worthy of being rescued from danger. We all crave meaning and often equate it with being part of a heroic story. The hero's quest is one of the oldest and most common tropes in literature because it resonates with our longing for significance.

But Jesus teaches us that our lives have meaning before we achieve any grand feats. True heroism is found not in self-promotion but in self-sacrifice. His example shows us that our worth isn't defined by how spectacularly we live but by the way we give ourselves in love and service.

The temptation to be powerful highlights our deep longing for control. Satan tempts Jesus by offering him the power to turn a stone into a loaf of bread, appealing to his immediate hunger during a time of fasting. The temptation is to take a shortcut, to satisfy his needs instantly. We all want what we want and we want it now, which is why patience is such a difficult virtue to cultivate.

Jesus reminds us that faith in God means trusting in the mystery of God's timing. We cannot force our lives into the shape we want through sheer willpower. Trusting God involves letting go of our need for control and learning to be content with life as it unfolds.

These temptations deceive us into thinking we can avoid the hard realities of life. In each case, we attempt to reclaim the power we feel we've lost, believing that with more control or agency, we could somehow make everything okay.

One of the hardest lessons in life is recognizing that we have far less power over our circumstances than we'd like to believe. True freedom begins when we relinquish the pursuit of power and surrender ourselves to God's ever-present and available grace. This surrender starts by naming and accepting the hard stuff in our lives. The pain, discomfort, heartache, and struggles are all parts of who we are. They are what we bring to a God who longs to welcome us, love us, and make us whole again.

The Power of Fear

Before we embark on the path to healing, we must first confront the most powerful of all dis-eases we carry—fear.

Fear is one of our primary human emotions. Psychologist Paul Ekman identifies it as one of the six core emotions shared across all cultures. It is a natural human response, helping us stay safe and avoid danger. Along with other primary emotions, fear brings clarity about our state of being.[3] To fully experience fear is to recognize that trouble lies ahead and to proceed with caution. It is both safe and natural to be afraid at times.

However, the dis-ease of fear is a different matter. It occurs when fear runs amok in our lives, extending far beyond a response to immediate threats. We start reacting to perceived dangers created in our own imaginations. Natural fear arises in response to real events; the dis-ease of fear responds to scenarios that are largely constructs of our minds.

Consider the fear that surfaces when you have a project deadline at work. The natural fear is tied to the reality of meeting that deadline—time passes whether we're ready or not. But the dis-ease of fear lurks beneath, feeding anxieties about what might happen if the deadline is missed: losing respect, missing future opportunities, or even losing your job. These fears are not based in reality but rather in the stories we tell ourselves.

Or think about a relationship that isn't going well. The other person seems perpetually unhappy, despite your best efforts to please them. The natural fear lies in facing the conflict and working toward resolution; after all, no one enjoys conflict. The dis-ease of fear, however, takes it a step further, leading us to worry about potential rejection or even the end of the relationship. It's the fear that we might end up alone or lose a significant source of meaning in our lives. We may not understand why things seem off until we actually engage with the other person, but that doesn't stop the dis-ease of fear from driving us down a path of worst-case scenarios. The reality could be that the other person is preoccupied with their own struggles (which may include their own mix of healthy and unhealthy fears), and that's why they haven't been able to engage in the relationship as fully.

The Big Book of Alcoholics Anonymous says we are "driven by a hundred forms of fear, self-delusion, self-seeking, and self-pity."[4] This fear causes us to lash out when things don't go our way, leading us to react impulsively and harbor resentment. It places

---

3. Guy-Evans, "Primary and Secondary Emotions."
4. *Alcoholics Anonymous*, 62.

ACCEPTING OURSELVES, GOOD, BAD, AND OTHERWISE

us in situations where we are more likely to be hurt, as we seek to control more than we should. Fear blinds us to truly listening to others; instead, we push our own agendas, convinced that we know what's best. We grow frustrated when people don't follow the plans we've laid out for them. In this way, fear leads us to play God in our own lives and in the lives of others, eventually leaving us angry when our authority goes unrecognized.

Fear is a dis-ease we cling to like a safety blanket. We think that as long as we're afraid, we can avoid danger at all costs. But fear also robs us of life—it keeps us from fully becoming the people God created us to be. It favors the safe path when risk could lead to new discoveries and insights. Though fear is hard to see, it is easy to feel. That's why it is crucial to dig deep and reflect, like a scavenger searching for hidden treasures, to uncover the fears lurking beneath the surface of our lives. We must find them and tell the truth about them if we are ever to overcome them.

Telling the Truth (to Ourselves and God)

Truth-telling is one of the greatest—and most difficult—gifts in life. It demands a delicate balance of courage and humility. Courage is needed to speak clearly and truthfully, while humility reminds us to restrain our clarity before it turns into a weapon against ourselves or others. There are many truths we must tell, even when they are hard to voice. But we must also discern when truth-telling crosses the line into intentionally causing harm.

An iconic image of Muhammad Ali captures him standing over George Foreman with his fist cocked as Foreman falls to the mat in the eighth round of one of their famous matches. Sometimes truth-telling is like that punch—necessary to confront the forces of abuse or oppression. Other times, it requires the restraint to hold back.

One of the most important lessons I've learned in recovery is that I cannot hope to tell the truth about the world around me until I first learn to tell the truth about the world within me. The clarity needed for truth-telling comes from examining and acknowledging the truth inside us. When we begin by trying to tell the truth about others, it's like adding a filter to a photo—you might see the truth, but it's distorted by your own unresolved issues, altering the picture.

In recovery we practice a process called personal inventory. This involves digging deep into who we are, recognizing our struggles, and identifying where negative patterns recur in our lives. We ask the question *why*—Why do these patterns persist, and how can we begin to change and break the cycles?

The personal inventory is a valuable tool for non-alcoholics as well, but it requires rigorous honesty. If you've reached the point where you're weary of the struggle (as discussed in chapter 1), and you're ready to surrender your life and will to God's love and care (as discussed in chapter 2), then you're prepared to take on the work of doing a personal inventory.

It's important to remember that God's grace is the foundation. Your desperation for change simply meets the grace that has always been available to you if only you would let go of trying to be the most powerful force in your life. Encountering that grace is profound, and doing a personal inventory, empowered by God's loving grace and your desire for change, marks the beginning of your response to God's love in your life.

The Big Book of Alcoholics Anonymous says we embark on this step by making "a searching and fearless moral inventory of ourselves."[5] Think of this process as a personal audit of your innermost being. Start by reflecting on the people or things you dislike or resent. Resentment is often a primary source of inner dis-ease because it acts like a parasite, feeding off anything it can. You may resent people who have wronged you, circumstances that didn't go your way, or situations where you felt treated unjustly. Some resentments will come to the surface easily, while others require deeper digging. There may even be hidden resentments you've convinced yourself don't exist, only to discover through prayer and a willingness to let God guide you that they are indeed present.

---

5. *Alcoholics Anonymous*, 59.

As a lifelong perfectionist, I struggled with resentment. I spent most of my life striving to be the very best at everything I did. When I couldn't achieve that, one of two things would happen:

First, I would blame others and resent whoever I believed was preventing me from proving myself. It could be a teacher who didn't recognize me as the smartest in the class, a girlfriend who didn't realize I was the best partner she could have, or a colleague who didn't defer to my ideas. If only they knew I had the answers to make life better! But deep down, their refusal to acknowledge my abilities felt like a statement about my worth—it was as if I wasn't good enough to be listened to, loved, or valued.

Second, I would turn the resentment inward and criticize myself. Why couldn't I measure up? Why didn't others see the potential in me that I saw, or wanted to see? When I failed, I became my harshest critic, convinced that not being the best meant I wasn't capable, smart, valuable, or even worthy. This emotional spiral was where alcohol became a coping mechanism—it helped numb the feelings of inadequacy and insecurity.

Making a list of your resentments can be a helpful step in processing and working through them, including the ways you resent yourself. The key is to be as honest as possible. Name the resentments, even if they're difficult to acknowledge. Be humble, too—you may wish you were over something and try to convince yourself that you are, yet still feel a nagging sense of it deep down. Have the courage to name it, and thank God for giving you that courage.

Naming your resentments helps you do something most of us find difficult. We may be skilled at identifying how others are wrong, but that's surface level. The deeper, more meaningful task is to identify how others make us feel and honestly examine our role in any conflict. In other words, redirect the focus from those you resent to yourself and ask what role you might have played and how you can grow beyond holding onto that resentment. Remember, you cannot control other people, but you can control how you respond to them.

After listing your resentments, explore the deeper reasons why they persist. Being mistreated is one thing, but understanding how that mistreatment triggers a deeper fear—a fear of not being loved, of lacking meaning, or of failing to meet expectations (whether your own or someone else's)—is something else entirely.

Learning to tell the truth about ourselves means learning to embrace our limitations. We spend so much of our lives trying to prove ourselves and deny our flaws. Yet, at the end of the day, we are simply human. This doesn't mean we are unworthy of love or incapable of achieving great things. It does mean, however, that we must recognize we cannot do everything or be everything for everyone. We are simply who we are, and that is enough. Being just who we are is also enough for God.

Getting Out of God's Way

The hardest thing I've ever attempted in my life of recovery is to let go of the things that hold me back—the fear, the moral defects, and the power of sin—and to ask God to take them away. That doesn't mean I don't continue to struggle with shortcomings and sin. But it does mean learning, day by day, to live more openhandedly with my life, even embracing my own brokenness. We ask God to take these burdens from us and then set out to do what seems emotionally impossible—to simply let go.

We learn to "drop the rock" and let God pick it up and carry it for us. If I'm prone to fear, I need to ask God to take the power of that fear from me *and* trust God to do it. It's one thing to ask God to work in our lives, but another to step aside and allow that work to happen. God cannot do God's work if I'm constantly managing and controlling everything. We may easily name the ways we fall short of being the people God calls us to be, but trusting God enough to surrender the power of those shortcomings is another matter altogether.

It may seem nearly impossible for you today, and that's okay. Your first prayer can simply be, "Help me be entirely willing to let go, O God." Praying for the willingness to let go will eventually lead to actual surrender. It's a wonderful mystery of faith. Trusting God with our lives, even the parts we struggle with, leads to a slow and miraculous transformation. We may not recognize the healing right away, but one day we'll notice a change and remember all those prayers for willingness. God was there all along, often just waiting for us to get out of the way.

In recovery, we talk about keeping our side of the emotional street clean. We cannot clean someone else's side. We may feel tempted to act like a neighborhood committee, judging others' emotional yards to see if they're up to standard. But a fundamental truth in embracing our powerlessness is realizing that we cannot judge whether others have a clean emotional street. Our task is to tend to our own emotional landscaping, letting go of the need to control or judge how others live their lives.

Letting go of trying to control others is really about releasing a burden. While our intentions may start from a place of love, over time that concern for others' well-being can take on distorted forms of control, judgment, or an unhealthy preoccupation with things that are not our business.

This is what we mean by "rightsizing" ourselves—learning to control only what we can and letting go of the rest. More importantly, releasing the burden of trying to control others frees up space for us to focus on awareness, growth, and healing within ourselves. We are the only ones we can control, and it takes a lifetime to examine the fears that live within us. It takes all our energy to name our shortcomings and limitations and to allow ourselves to be human. Learning to truly love ourselves is a monumental task made possible only through God's grace and our response of surrendering to that grace—letting go of what occupies too much space in our souls and prevents that grace from taking root.

Kintsugi is an ancient art that mends broken objects with gold. The word comes from the Japanese *kin* (gold) and *tsugi* (join), literally meaning "golden joinery." The art form is called *kintsukuroi*, or "mending with gold." It serves as a beautiful metaphor for the work of personal inventory: naming and embracing our fears and limitations, and getting out of God's way so that God can take charge of our lives. Embracing what we've spent much of our lives trying to hide is a risky endeavor. It's a risk that others might discover we're not as powerful as we want them to think we are, and it's a risk that we might occasionally fail or fall short of expectations.

The good news is that faith in Jesus often leads us to places we never thought we could go. Instead of preserving our lives at all costs, Jesus calls us to lay them down for the sake of others. To gain true wealth, we are called to give ourselves away. And to know the true power of God at work in our lives, we must embrace our weaknesses. Paul reminds us that when he prayed from a place of weakness, God said to him, "My grace is sufficient for you, for power is made perfect in weakness." With that assurance, Paul was able to say, "I will boast all the more gladly of my weaknesses, so that the power of Christ may dwell in me."[6]

It is from this place of healing that we begin some of the most fundamental and life-changing work possible—learning the art of forgiveness.

---

6. 2 Cor 12:9.

Chapter 4: Accepting and Giving Forgiveness

Not forgiving is like drinking rat poison and then waiting for the rat to die.[1]

—Anne Lamott

WITH THE FOUNDATION LAID—EMBRACING our powerlessness, rightsizing ourselves to fully surrender to God, and examining our inner selves to address the fears and resentments we carry—we are now ready to apply these foundational lessons to areas of life common to all of us.

In the next few chapters, we'll explore how to grow in handling conflict and practicing forgiveness, learn to love our families better (or simply coexist in them more peacefully), parent our children, thrive in our careers without being consumed by work, and live in a way that shares the love and grace we've come to know with others.

Needing Forgiveness

All human beings hurt other human beings. It's part of our fallen nature. As someone once said, "Humans will human from time

---

1. Lamott, *Traveling Mercies*, 134.

to time." Our pursuit of self-preservation inevitably collides with someone else's, and when this happens, conflict arises. Most conflicts require one or both parties to admit they were wrong and seek or grant forgiveness.

We learn this reality early in life, perhaps on the playground, when someone doesn't play fair and ruins the game for others. Or as adolescents coming of age, we might do almost anything to fit into a cool group at school. Then, one day, the group starts mocking a good friend, and a moment of truth presents itself—either stand up for the friend or join in to fit in. Before we know it, we've hurt someone we care about.

Married couples hurt each other more often than they care to admit. One partner might overreact or lie to protect their self-interest, whether it's about forgetting a promise or redirecting frustration from an unrelated situation. If the mistake goes unnoticed, things may blow over. But when the other person recognizes what's happening or asserts that they deserve more consideration, conflict ensues. Good communicators may address it by naming the hurt and seeking forgiveness, but most of us struggle to navigate the process of forgiveness smoothly.

Even knowing how to apologize can be challenging, as it often becomes self-serving. When our partner expresses hurt, we may get defensive:

- "I didn't mean to do that . . . you shouldn't be so sensitive!"
- Or we deflect with a quid pro quo: "Well, you did ___, so what did you expect?"
- Sometimes, we lie to cover up our mistakes, letting one small lie compound into more, all to protect our self-image.

Parents hurt their children, too. As kids, we often view adults with a certain mythical awe—they seem smart, responsible, and capable. But as we grow up, we learn that those adults were simply flawed human beings, doing the best they could with what they knew.

ACCEPTING AND GIVING FORGIVENESS

Even the way we are taught to love can be imperfect. Parents often love their children as they themselves need to be loved, repeating patterns learned from their upbringing. While most healthy parents have a deep love for their children, that love is also shaped by the way they were taught—whether positive or negative. This means a parent's love is both deep and imperfect, and part of growing up is learning to break cycles of hurt from our past. The ways we were loved (or not) growing up influence how we love throughout life. If we were loved with healthy boundaries and selflessness, we are more likely to pass that on. If we experienced conditional love, guilt, neglect, or shame, we may need to heal from those early experiences to love others in better ways.

Hurting one another is, unfortunately, part of the human experience. The Lord's Prayer reminds us to ask God to "forgive us our trespasses as we forgive those who trespass against us." This might sound like a conditional statement, implying that if we don't forgive, then God won't forgive us. But what if it points to a deeper, more mysterious understanding of forgiveness? What if the conditional nature we perceive is rooted not in God's character, but in our own flawed experiences of love and forgiveness?

Help us forgive others, O God, as you have forgiven us. If we forgive as we've been taught by others, our understanding of forgiveness may be shallow and limited. That's why we must learn a more perfect forgiveness from God. Human forgiveness is often conditional and flawed, while God's forgiveness sets a higher standard, inviting us to move beyond our limited human perspectives.

To understand forgiveness more deeply, start by making a list of people you've hurt. Reflect on the ways you've wronged them and own your role in their pain. It's a humbling and freeing process. When you feel ready, consider reaching out to these people, one by one, to make amends. Remember, making amends isn't about pointing out what they did wrong—it's about owning your part in the hurt. The goal is to release the guilt you carry by coming clean to the person you hurt. Whether they choose to forgive you is not up to you; your freedom comes from taking responsibility and giving them the space to respond as they choose.

Forgiveness requires trusting God above all. Our primary task is to offer amends without attaching conditions, which frees us from trying to control the other person and allows the work of healing to remain where it belongs—in God's hands.

The forgiveness we seek and the forgiveness we offer are two sides of the same coin. We need both giving and receiving forgiveness to fully grasp its healing power. So we lay bare our brokenness, flaws, and the ways we've hurt others as we now explore how God might be drawing us into deeper healing through learning to forgive.

Forgiving Others

Who has hurt you? Maybe it's a minor, everyday misunderstanding or the typical human squabbles that are easily resolved. But I'd be willing to bet that most of us carry a deeper, uglier hurt. It's the kind of hurt that's sensitive to the touch and leaves lasting scars. It lives in the deep places of our souls, weighing us down with pain, doubt, and insecurity. It's often the secret hurts that burden us the most.

I once read a story that really resonated with me about what it means to forgive but not forget. Two siblings are discussing their feelings about their dad who recently died. Kevin tells his sister he doesn't excuse the abuse they endured, but he's managed to forgive their father. His sister Kate is shocked. She's so overwhelmed with anger she can't imagine ever forgiving. Hearing the loathing in her voice, Kevin hugs Kate and gently explains that holding onto her rage means their father still has the power—the abuse continues to harm her.[2]

Even though he has forgiven, Kevin never tells Kate to "forgive and forget" or that what happened to them doesn't matter. "If we forget our personal or our world's history, we risk having cycles of

---

2. See Hazelden Betty Ford Foundation, "Forgiveness."

abuse and injustice repeat themselves."³ He knows Kate has reason to be angry, and he listens while she talks about her pain.

Much like admitting our powerlessness over life, we must name our hurts if we want them to have a fighting chance to heal. The process of naming our pain becomes harder and messier the closer we are to the person who hurt us. Naming the hurt inflicted by a schoolyard bully is very different from naming the hurt caused by a parent, spouse, or trusted adult in our childhood.

> **Important Note:** *I must emphasize the importance of seeking help from a licensed professional to navigate the weight of these hurts. I have been in therapy for years, and I cannot overstate the difference it has made in my life. There's no way I could have sorted through the complexities of my life and past on my own.*

I'll never forget my pastor telling me after my dad left that it was okay not to fully forgive him right away. She said I was only obligated to forgive him as much as I could at that moment. She suggested I pray, asking God to make up the difference between what I was able to forgive and what was needed for full forgiveness.

I wish I could say I remained faithful to that prayer over the years. Eventually, though, I reached a point where I saw his leaving as more of a symptom of his own struggles with mental and emotional health. He didn't set out to hurt us intentionally, but he did make choices that prioritized his own desires over his family. On the one hand, he didn't know what else to do. On the other, that didn't make leaving the right choice. This tension helped me remember that we are all doing the best we can with the light we have. It also served as a powerful reminder that being a father and husband is a tall order and a heavy responsibility—not a role to abandon just because it gets difficult.

The most challenging moments in relationships are often the times when I need to turn inward and examine the state of my own soul. What fear is quietly controlling me and causing me to question who God calls me to be as a husband and father? What

---

3. Hazelden Betty Ford Foundation, "Forgiveness."

insecurity is clouding my vision, making me lose sight of what truly matters? These difficult moments usually indicate something within me that needs addressing—even if it means letting go of my need to control those I love most and giving them the freedom to be their own people.

I had to forgive my dad to release the burden of resentment I carried. It was the only way to find freedom in my own life.

Holding onto unforgiveness and resentment ultimately harms us more than anyone else. Anne Lamott describes earth as a sort of "forgiveness school," where we learn how to deal with the hurts we experience and those we inflict on others. She suggests that it's best to start practicing forgiveness at the dinner table with the people closest to us—where we can learn while wearing comfy pants.[4]

Forgiving others doesn't come easy, nor does it happen immediately. It requires time and effort. Sometimes, the most forgiveness we can offer is simply resolving in our own hearts not to carry the burden of resentment any longer. Whatever we do, healing should be the destination we strive for, with God as our guide, giving us the strength needed for this difficult journey.

Living Beyond the Hurt

Whatever your motivation—whether it's to escape the heavy burden of resentment, to finally let go of the nagging obligation of holding a grudge, or simply to have an excuse to wear comfy pants—life is best lived when we learn to move beyond the hurt and pain we carry. This doesn't erase the past, but it does make space for the pain to loosen its grip on us.

I once saw an image of a mason jar with a tennis ball inside, sitting next to a larger jar with the same-sized tennis ball. In the smaller jar, the ball took up most of the space, while in the larger jar, it seemed much smaller in proportion. This is how life with grief and pain often feels—it's not that the pain ever completely

---

4. Lamott, "12 Truths," 9:59–10:12.

ACCEPTING AND GIVING FORGIVENESS

disappears, but that we grow to make more room for life without it consuming all the free space in our souls.

Resentment robs the soul, inevitably leading to unhappiness and cutting us off from fully living in the light of God's grace. True forgiveness is a process. It's not easy to let go of such heavy burdens, especially when resentment has begun to eat away at us from the inside out.

The good news is that freedom from the burden of resentment is possible, even without participation from the person you resent. Working through this process can reconnect us with others or even with parts of ourselves that become lost when bitterness and resentment take over.

Back to our story about Kevin and Kate. What made Kevin capable of forgiveness was learning he could feel anger about the abuse he and his sister suffered without letting his father's actions prevent him from healing. "Forgiveness can exist simultaneously with anger, just as joy can exist in the midst of grief." However, rushing to forgive before being ready can be "a compulsive attempt at peacemaking done with no processing of emotion and no coming to terms with the injury," which is "premature, superficial, and undeserved."[5]

We can't change the past—and admitting that is the first step toward forgiving. Forgiveness frees us from the bitterness that stands in the way of experiencing true joy in life. Saying we're sorry just to move on isn't healthy; forgiveness is a process that takes time and cannot be short-circuited. We must move through it one day at a time.[6]

And perhaps the person you need to forgive most is yourself.

Somewhere in early development, we learn to be self-conscious. Healthy self-consciousness serves as a safety mechanism, helping us adapt to our surroundings, behave appropriately in groups, determine what should be shared or kept private, and examine ourselves critically to ensure we feel safe and connected.

---

5. Hazelden Betty Ford Foundation, "Forgiveness."
6. See Hazelden Betty Ford Foundation, "Forgiveness."

But there's a fine line between healthy and unhealthy self-consciousness. It takes trial and error to calibrate it into a balanced, mature state. This balance is a learned understanding that comes with growth, experience, and God's grace.

Shame is a hallmark of the unhealthy side of self-consciousness, and it becomes even more damaging when used as a weapon. You may have had a parent, spouse, or loved one who wielded shame to control you. It's a powerful tool because its effects linger long after the person who used it is gone. To heal, we must reclaim our dignity and develop a healthy sense of self-worth, refusing to let shame dictate what we do, how we feel, or what we think.

So to all you perfectionists and those who have been victims of shame-wielding, this is your permission: There is hope for you, too, when you begin to forgive yourself and let go of the power shame has held over you.

The good news is that the way toward healing is marked with compassion. Henri Nouwen writes, "The great illusion of leadership is to think that man can be led out of the desert by someone who has never been there."[7] Real healing begins not only when we let go of the burden of our resentment or shame, but when those very burdens become tools for offering love and compassion to others—and also to ourselves. Painful experiences soften and shape our hearts, making them more malleable. They also provide us with opportunities to recognize when others are going through a similar pain, enabling us to be more gracious with ourselves and others as we learn to hold our past hurts tenderly.

There's an old fable that illustrates this well: A man is out for a walk when he trips and falls into a deep hole. The hole is so deep he can't crawl out, so he shouts for anyone who can hear him, "Help! Please, I've fallen in a hole!" A psychiatrist walks by and drops a sample of anti-anxiety medication down to the man. Then a pastor comes by and tosses the man a prayer book to help alleviate his spiritual stress. The guy takes the pill, reads some prayers, then looks around, feeling hopeless, still in the bottom of the hole. Finally, a friend, hearing his cries for help, comes running. Before

---

7. Nouwen, *Wounded Healer*, 72.

the man can say a word, the friend has made his way to the bottom of the hole right along with him. The man says, "You're crazy! Now both of us are stuck in this pit!" The friend smiles and says, "Yeah, but I've taken the same tumble. I know this hole. And together we can find our way back to the light."

No matter why you are in the hole, there is a way out. It's a path marked by forgiveness, healing, and compassion for others. It reminds us that we are never truly alone, even in our deepest hurts. Guilt, shame, and resentment don't have to control our lives. We can name them courageously and begin to release them, with God's help, one day at a time.

Chapter 5: Accepting Our Families of Origin

Happiness is having a large, loving, caring, close-knit family in another city.

—GEORGE BURNS

DYSFUNCTIONAL FAMILIES HAVE EXISTED since the dawn of time. This truth is evident from the very beginning, shortly after Adam and Eve are exiled from the garden of Eden. Sin enters the human condition and immediately begins to manifest in their family life. The book of Genesis alone is filled with examples of just how dysfunctional families can be, offering patterns of dysfunction that resonate with families throughout history who struggle to be healthy.

Cain and Abel—Sibling Rivalry

Genesis 4:1–5 tells us that Adam and Eve had two sons, Cain and Abel. Abel was a shepherd, while Cain worked the land. When it came time to make offerings to God, Cain brought some of the firstfruits of the earth, while Abel presented the firstborn of his flock as a sacrifice. The story goes that God looked favorably on Abel's offering but not on Cain's, leaving Cain feeling angry and dejected.

Sibling rivalry is as old as time itself. From the moment we enter the world, we compete for our parents' full attention. For firstborn children, the arrival of siblings means that the attention they once enjoyed gets divided. Parents only have so much time and energy to give, and the competition between siblings can become more intense if parents don't always parent in healthy ways. Children may end up feeling as though they must compete for their parents' love, leading to resentment—especially if one child consistently feels like they're on the losing end.

Cain didn't know how to manage his anger and disappointment, so he directed it outward, taking it out on Abel rather than dealing with it internally. By Gen 4:8, we witness the first murder in Scripture. While most of us may not want to kill our siblings, the resentment we harbor when we feel they receive more love and attention can certainly stir some intense emotions.

An often overlooked aspect of this family dysfunction is how Adam and Eve, rather than truly addressing the trauma of losing a child, had another son, Seth. They essentially declared him the replacement for their lost child. It's common for families who have experienced loss to rush to replace whatever it is they lost. It's a way to minimize their pain instead. But replacing our loss often comes at the expense of confronting and potentially healing the emotional trauma and sin within the family. In this context, replacement becomes a way to manage grief—a grief that is always proportional to the unresolved emotional residue left by the losses we endure. Adam, instead of processing the grief of losing Abel and the pain of knowing his other son was responsible, tried to move on by viewing Seth as a substitute for Abel.

Abraham and Sarah—Trying to Play God in Our Families

Another example of a dysfunctional family in the Bible is Abraham's. Though now regarded as the foundation of the Jewish, Christian, and Muslim traditions, their family dynamics were far from ideal.

In Gen 15, God makes a covenant with Abraham, promising protection and a lasting lineage. Abraham reminds God that he has yet to have children with Sarah, but God reassures him that his descendants will one day outnumber the stars in the sky. However, this promise required patience, and, like many of us, Abraham and Sarah struggled to wait.

Genesis 16 recounts the birth of Ishmael, born to Sarah's slave, Hagar, as a result of their impatience. Assuming Sarah would never conceive, they used Hagar to fulfill their desire for a child, disregarding her personhood and exploiting her simply for her ability to bear children.

By Gen 18, God reveals that Sarah would indeed conceive, and in Gen 21 we see the tragic consequences of Hagar's exploitation: Hagar and Ishmael are banished by Abraham and Sarah, who now have a son of their own. While God provides for Hagar and Ishmael, it is despite Abraham and Sarah's manipulations, not because of them.

Abraham and Sarah's story is timeless and sadly still relevant today. Families sometimes exploit or abuse members, keeping them around only as long as they serve a purpose and discarding them once that purpose is fulfilled.

The real dysfunction in Abraham and Sarah's story isn't just their impatience or lack of faith—it's their belief that they are at the center of the universe, with everything and everyone existing solely to meet their needs. They mistakenly think that God's promise makes them exceptional, giving them the freedom to use others at will. Quietly and subtly, they make the same mistake many of us do—they try to play God instead of trusting the God of the universe.

Jacob's Big Dysfunctional Family

A third biblical example of family dysfunction is found in the story of Jacob, later known as Israel. His family serves as a case study in triangulation, emotional cutoff, and lack of differentiation. In

ACCEPTING OUR FAMILIES OF ORIGIN

many ways, Jacob's family mirrors our own, reflecting the layers of dysfunction that often play out in our lives.

Genesis 29-30 recounts the competitive struggle between Leah and Rachel for Jacob's affection, leading to the birth of many of Jacob's children not only through Leah and Rachel but also their maidservants. The tension between Leah and Rachel exemplifies a classic triangulated relationship, where their rivalry draws the children into the conflict. According to Bowen family systems theory, triangulation occurs when two people in conflict involve a third person to stabilize their relationship, often resulting in greater dysfunction within the family.[1]

Jacob's favoritism toward Joseph is evident in Gen 37:3-4, where he gives Joseph a "coat of many colors," sparking deep resentment among his brothers. Jacob's inability to differentiate his feelings for Rachel and her children from those for his other children creates significant family tension. This favoritism ultimately leads Joseph's brothers to plot against him, demonstrating the destructive impact of Jacob's emotional imbalance within the family.

Lack of differentiation, or enmeshment, is a common family dysfunction. Differentiation refers to the process by which individuals develop a strong sense of self while maintaining emotional connections with their family. Without differentiation, family members may struggle to establish healthy boundaries, becoming overly dependent on or entangled in each other's emotions, decisions, and well-being. This lack of emotional separation can result in conflicts and unresolved tension, as personal identity becomes lost within the family unit.[2]

Establishing our own identity, separate from the family unit we come from, is one of the most challenging tasks we face. It's a point I often stress in premarital counseling: when you create a new family you must emotionally leave your families of origin behind to make this new family your primary focus. For parents, this process can be just as difficult, if not more so. They may use financial or emotional support to keep their children from fully

---

1. Kerr and Bowen. *Family Evaluation*, 134-40.
2. Kerr and Bowen. *Family Evaluation*, 97-103.

"flying the nest," subtly maintaining control and preventing the formation of an independent family unit.

In more extreme cases, families experience emotional cutoff. Bowen describes emotional cutoff as a coping mechanism used to manage unresolved emotional issues with family members by reducing or entirely severing emotional contact. This often occurs when individuals feel overwhelmed by unresolved tension or pain, leading them to distance themselves from family rather than address the underlying issues. Joseph's brothers' decision to sell him into slavery and deceive Jacob into believing Joseph was dead (Gen 37:28–35) is a classic example of emotional cutoff. In an attempt to cope with their jealousy and hatred they sever emotional ties with Joseph, using the drastic act of selling him as a way to distance themselves from the unresolved tension in the family. Instead of addressing their feelings, they choose to cut him out of their lives entirely.

The stories of Cain and Abel, Abraham and Sarah, and Jacob's family in Genesis illustrate core principles of family systems theory, showing how unresolved emotional issues, favoritism, and generational patterns can lead to deep family dysfunction. These biblical families reflect the complicated dynamics many of us encounter in our own families of origin. While not all of these challenges can be easily solved, healing becomes possible when we have the courage to face these truths and open ourselves to God's guidance on our journey toward greater self-awareness.

Mapping a Family Genogram

Families are complex systems shaped by multiple interconnected factors. A genogram is a visual representation of a family tree that goes beyond the basic structure of lineage, providing important insights into the relationships between family members. It serves as a valuable tool for understanding the psychological, emotional, and hereditary factors that shape individuals and families. Genograms use symbols to depict various characteristics, including gender, relationships, emotions, instances of abuse, diseases, genetic predispositions, and other factors that influence family dynamics.[3] To understand your family well, you must know the dynamics of the various relationships across generations.

Families can be a mixed bag. They offer many positives—people who love us, support us, provide for us, and inspire us. But they also carry less favorable elements. Stories of failure, shame, or trauma can shape a family tree, and patterns of abuse or dysfunction can quietly shift family dynamics for generations.

Edwin Friedman emphasizes the importance of avoiding linear thinking when analyzing family trees. He argues that family relationships are not simple one-to-one interactions; they are influenced by the entire family system, with multiple factors shaping each connection. For example, your relationship with your mother is affected by:

- Your mother's relationship with her parents (especially her relationship with her own mother, according to Friedman)
- Your mother's relationship with her spouse, if there is another adult present
- Your relationship with that other adult in the household
- The presence and influence of siblings[4]

These interconnected relationships demonstrate how family systems impact each individual connection, making it impossible to understand one relationship in isolation. In other words, every family has dynamics that affect each relationship. You cannot separate a single connection from the surrounding dynamics, as these factors inevitably shape it.

Friedman encourages us to think in terms of systems rather than simple, linear cause and effect. By viewing families this way, we can better understand the complexities of relationships and how they are shaped by the entire family unit.[5]

---

3. NeuroLaunch, "Genogram Emotional Relationship Symbols."
4. Friedman, *Generation to Generation*, 15.
5. Friedman, *Generation to Generation*, 17.

Every family has dynamics that impact each relationship. You cannot isolate a single relationship from the surrounding dynamics, as these factors inevitably influence it. Friedman encourages us to think in terms of systems rather than simple, linear cause and effect. Viewing families this way allows us to better understand the complexities of relationships and how they are shaped by the entire family unit.

This shift in thinking is especially useful when examining the "sick" elements of our families—those parts of the family tree that include stories of abuse, addiction, or other struggles. While it may be tempting to isolate these sick elements, a comprehensive analysis of the entire family and their responses to these issues is necessary to understand the full complexity of family dynamics.

For example, my father suffers from mental illness. He is bipolar and battles severe bouts of mania and depression. As a child, I remember him withdrawing for days at a time, becoming increasingly quiet and isolated from the family. This had a profound impact on me because, when he was well, he was my best friend. As a seven- or eight-year-old, I felt confused when he would refuse to throw the football with me, saying he couldn't play because he felt sick and needed to sit in his chair. He didn't look sick. He didn't sound sick.

It wasn't until years later that I understood how his depression could render him almost immobile. For a long time, I blamed him for emotionally neglecting me and my sister. His departure when I was twelve felt like the culmination of years of withdrawal. I saw myself as a victim of his illness, collateral damage in a battle he seemed to be losing.

It took me about thirty years to realize that the trauma of a broken home during my adolescence was far more complex than just a story of a father who failed his children. When I map out my family genogram, I see other factors influencing our tumultuous family dynamics:

- My father grew up with an abusive, alcoholic father, which left him without a healthy example of how to love as a father.

- My mother grew up in a home where she lost a sibling at a young age. This trauma influenced her parenting style, leading to a focus on family survival and leaving little room for emotional expression. In her view, every family member had a role to play, and survival was the top priority.

I could delve even deeper by analyzing their relationships with their siblings, but the point is clear: Family dynamics are far more complex than straightforward, one-to-one relationships. By mapping these intricate connections in a genogram, we gain a deeper understanding of the multifaceted influences within our families, leading to potentially greater insights and healing.

Now that we recognize our families as complex systems of relationships, dynamics, and emotions, it's crucial to examine the scripts we follow to navigate these systems.

Untangling and Finding New Scripts

I came of age watching sitcoms from the 1980s and 1990s. My absolute favorites were the family sitcoms on ABC's TGIF lineup. Each family was unique, filled with distinct characters, and every character displayed their own quirks in how they related to other family members. The scripts emphasized these differences for comedic effect.

While sitcoms exaggerate characters for laughs, they also reveal something deeper about families. Every member of a family is a distinct character within the family system. Each person has their own way of relating to others, and every family seems to follow a script—an unspoken, guiding narrative that shapes how they function as a unit.

In my family, our script was all about survival. We faced major setbacks, especially with my father. After he left, survival became the driving force behind everything we did. Any choice or desire was measured by how it contributed to keeping the family unit intact.

What was the script you learned growing up? Was your family close-knit, where love was openly shared? Or was there a colder atmosphere? Did your family express love in healthy ways, empowering you to grow into an emotionally healthy adult? Or was the family script tangled with complexities and secrets? Are you a survivor of childhood trauma—physical, emotional, or verbal abuse?

One of the hardest—but most important—things we can do as adults is to revisit and untangle the scripts we learned growing up. This isn't about harsh judgment; rather, it's about understanding those scripts so we can decide which elements still serve us well and which are best left behind. Most family scripts develop over time with good intentions—to share love and help each other thrive. But since we are all human, those scripts often have flaws.

It's crucial to remember that people—like our parents and their parents—were doing the best they could with the light they had. Extending grace as we examine the ways these scripts shaped us, for better or worse, can be transformative.

> **Important Note:** Abuse is real, and none of this is meant to excuse the harm caused when people are victimized. If there is abuse in your family history, the goal is not to excuse it but to understand its roots. It's like turning a kaleidoscope to view the situation from all its angles and complexities. If you have experienced abuse in your family, seeking help from a professional is crucial.

It's funny how much children mimic their parents. I'm not entirely sure where nature (our DNA) ends and nurture (learned patterns of behavior) begins, but the influence of both can profoundly impact our lives and the lives of future generations—for better or for worse.

Substance abuse runs on both sides of my family. While not all of it has been diagnosed, it's present. There is undoubtedly a component of my alcoholism that is inherited. However, I know that's not an excuse to remain in active addiction. Blaming my DNA doesn't bring healing; if anything, it's an excuse to continue patterns that are destructive to myself and those I love most.

I also grew up in a family where perfectionism was the norm. We were always expected to mind our p's and q's, were held to the high standards we set for ourselves, and were never supposed to falter. We dressed in our Sunday best for church and strived to be seen as respectable, successful people in all we did. But these habits don't have to foster an unhealthy expression of perfectionism in me.

Some of the scripts we live by are embedded in our DNA, while others are patterns of learned behavior reinforced throughout childhood. This doesn't make any of them inherently good or bad—they simply are. As adults striving for healing, our work is to recognize these influences, tell the truth about them, and examine them so we can begin living into our true selves, beyond the roles and perceptions shaped by our family scripts.

This is also true in how we show love and interact with one another. Some of us grew up in homes where love had to be earned, while others experienced love as controlling, stifling our ability to grow and differentiate as children should. No parent is perfect, and we can acknowledge that while also striving to break the patterns that affected us negatively, ensuring we don't repeat the mistakes of the past.

Edwin Friedman notes that it takes three generations to truly understand family dynamics. Children are influenced by their grandparents, largely through the ways their parents were raised.[6] We're shaped by our DNA, but we also absorb behavior patterns based on upbringing. When combined with how we relate to those closest to us, these influences create a complex life script that we begin learning at a young age. These scripts can be passed down through generations, often without us realizing it. While they can serve us well, they can also cause harm. For most of us, they probably do a bit of both.

Family scripts come in all shapes and sizes, and we must learn to see them in perspective—rightsized, just as we learn to see ourselves. This doesn't minimize the trauma we experience; rather, it

---

6. Friedman, *Generation to Generation*, 18.

means that we don't have to let that trauma define us. It takes hard work, prayer, and often professional help to reach this point.

Breaking generational cycles is one of the most profound gifts we can give our children. History doesn't have to repeat itself. DNA doesn't have to dictate patterns of neglect, abuse, or trauma. Transformation is possible through the grace of God. Embracing powerlessness, rightsizing ourselves, surrendering to God's love and care, and doing the work of self-examination to weed out our fears and resentments—all of this can help us flip the script in our lives, not just for our sake but for the sake of generations to come.

Chapter 6: Accepting Our Role as Healthy Parents

Having children is like living in a frat house—nobody sleeps, everything's broken, and there's a lot of throwing up.

—RAY ROMANO

The Wonder of Parenthood

PARENTHOOD IS BOTH THE hardest and greatest thing in my life. I often share this with new parents. It's incredible, amazing, and even mind-blowing to be a parent. I remember when my daughter was born and we were sent home after a couple of days—no instruction manual, no pediatric nurse to guide us. They just said congrats and sent us on our way. Luckily, I married a pediatric nurse whose mother was a neonatal nurse, so I was fairly confident we wouldn't accidentally harm this newborn creature. Still, it's remarkable that we send wide-eyed, inexperienced adults home every day with newborns and expect them to know how to love and raise these tiny beings.

I didn't want kids of my own for a very long time. I don't know if I've ever told my children that (although I guess they'll read it now). But I was terrified to become a parent. Growing up, my house was not an easy place. My parents lived in constant tension. If it wasn't an all-out screaming match, it was a low-level disdain that lingered in the air. I vividly remember walking on eggshells whenever all four of us were home at the same time, knowing that a fight could break out at any moment, filling the day with conflict. We weren't a tender family. We didn't share feelings openly. The unspoken directive was to "do your job"—whether that meant earning money for the family to survive or going to school and making good grades because "you don't waste your God-given intelligence." Our family operated by living up to expectations and not disrupting the delicate rhythm of the household.

My dad left in 1994 after a mental health breakdown that led him to attempt suicide. He worked the night shift as a police officer and slept during the day while we were at school and my mom was at work. We had a woman who helped us get ready for school, serving as a bridge between us and two parents who were often like ships passing in the night. I remember my aunt checking me out of school the day my dad attempted suicide. She took us to her house, which was very out of the ordinary. While we were close, she was never an after-school option. I was too young to suspect anything was wrong. That evening, my mom sat us down and explained that my dad was in the hospital after taking some expired medication before his daily nap. His plan was to exit this world peacefully, leaving his struggles—and us—behind. Not long after, he left the family to move back to his home state where he sought to address his mental health issues. I don't know if he ever fully sorted it all out, and our family never truly processed the impact his departure had on us.

After he left, the expectations tightened as we reformed ourselves from a family of four to a family of three. My mom worked tirelessly, sacrificing a great deal to ensure we survived on her single income. My sister and I took on the role of supporting those sacrifices. Our "jobs" became doing well in school and staying out of trouble. I can still feel the thickness of the tension at times—one wrong move, and it seemed like our family would unravel at the seams. I always admired my younger sister because she never let that tension prevent her from being her own person, free to express herself. I never felt that freedom. I was too afraid of disappointing everyone, so I kept my feelings to myself and let my productivity speak for itself. I focused on achievement and fulfilling my role to help our family thrive.

As I grew into adulthood, I realized this wasn't the healthiest way to grow up. We did the best we could given the circumstances, but, looking back, I feel that, despite my academic intelligence, I was a few years behind in the school of emotional health. I didn't learn how to express my feelings openly or accept my limitations. Much of my childhood was accelerated after my father's suicide attempt. I thought it was a badge of honor to assume the role of man of the house, not realizing the tremendous amount of undue pressure that title placed on me—something no child should ever bear.

I loved being married. It's an incredible gift to be loved by another human being. But I wasn't sure I wanted children. I don't know if I even knew how to voice the fear I had about being a parent. I was afraid of failing my kids, of not knowing how to be a good father. The only example I had was a loving man whose love was complicated by mental health issues and an unhappy marriage—complications that eventually severed his relationship with his kids.

One of the greatest wonders I can name about being a parent is how God's grace shows up in such preemptive and surprising ways. I don't know that I ever consciously chose to love my children before I was captivated by their very being. Both of my kids struggled to sleep through the night (my daughter much more than my son), and I often had solo night shifts because my wife worked as a night nurse. I remember waking up for the second or third time each night to tend to a crying baby. I was exhausted, angry, and just praying for a reprieve from the crying and constant sleep interruptions. But as soon as I entered their room, a power greater than myself would inevitably take over. I would hold them, try to console them, and find myself quietly captivated by their presence all over again.

Watching children grow into their own people is a wonder-filled experience. Learning to walk and talk are amazing milestones, but watching them find interests, make friends, and begin navigating a life uniquely their own is on a whole other level. Most days I still don't know if I'm doing this fatherhood thing right. But with God's help, a tremendous amount of therapy, and learning to go back and heal those early wounds, I believe I'm slowly becoming the father I would have wanted as a kid. And that, in itself, is one of the most healing gifts I could ever ask for in this life.

Before I delve into my views on fatherhood and manhood, I want to explain why I write less about motherhood. Obviously, I don't know what that experience is like. I have a wonderful wife who is an amazing mother, and I know many friends and examples of motherhood in my life. In many ways being a mother is similar to being a father—trying to balance work, home, and keeping these precious beings alive and well-adjusted. But I also recognize that mothers, and women in general, carry a different set of burdens and expectations.

Having never been a mother myself, I don't want to pretend to be an expert. I have a good mother, though imperfect like all mothers. I also recognize the privilege of being a man and a father, where societal expectations tend to be lower than those placed on mothers. So the next sections are not meant to exclude women but to help us understand the complexities men bring into our lives as we all try to figure out the best ways to be human.

The Complexities of Fatherhood

My relationship with my father—or lack thereof—has had a tremendous impact on my life, for better or worse. Even if you're not a father, your relationship with your own father (or lack thereof) might be weighing on you in various ways.

When I say the word *father*, what images come to mind? Maybe you remember a wonderful father in your life, or perhaps you think of TV dads who shaped early images of fatherhood—sitcom dads who worked hard and tried to be present for their families but often stumbled as husbands and struggled to understand their kids.

Or perhaps your memories of fathers are marked by absence. Some fathers are physically absent, leaving their families to pursue different lives. Others may be emotionally absent—physically present, but never truly attentive to their children's emotional needs.

Whatever complicated image arises, it's clear that what it means to be a man, and by extension a father, has been in flux for a couple of generations.

For many generations, the hallmark of manhood and fatherhood was the role of provider. This stereotype goes back centuries, with men seen as hunters or workers who provided for the family, while women, having borne the children, were considered natural nurturers who ran the household. Mid-twentieth-century America seemed to embody this division of labor. In a Norman Rockwell vision of American life, fathers were depicted as strong but emotionally distant, while mothers were submissive yet loving.

The problem with these stereotypes is that they rarely held up in creating emotionally healthy families. Families need environments where needs are met, individuals are empowered to be self-aware, and love is freely shared.

Fatherhood—and manhood, for that matter—is as unique and nuanced as every human being who seeks to embody the role. We often project our own insecurities, believing we must be stewards of all truth. The reality is that many men are unsure how to be a man or a father, and they desperately seek answers wherever they can find them. The truth is, there is no single way to be a man or a father. All we can do is the best we can with the light we have. But when we adhere to fictionalized notions of "being a man"—the tough guy image that modern society promotes—we risk hiding our true selves behind a façade. The best thing a man can do to be a good father is to be himself, inside and out, to the very best of his ability, with the help of God.

To be a father is to learn to love beyond yourself. The modern image of macho men who emphasize toughness is often a projection of the little boys living inside every man. These little boys have common fears—of being accepted, of feeling enough, of needing to be loved in return. Outward expressions of a tough persona act like a Teflon shield, protecting the vulnerable little boy within.

Being a father means coming to terms with that inner child and his needs. Loving your children becomes a way to learn to love your inner self. The grace of it all is that it's reciprocal—the more we learn to love ourselves honestly, the more we can love our children genuinely. As we grow on this lifelong journey, Teflon exteriors and macho personas become meaningless. We learn to simply be who we are and love from a deep reservoir of grace that comes from not being afraid to know ourselves.

Our views on fatherhood and motherhood are imperfect at best. The expectations we place on these roles shape men and women profoundly as they parent. Moreover, the ways we live into these roles influence the future, as we do our best to guide our children with the light we have.

Being a father is a uniquely beautiful role that can have a tremendous impact on the next generation. For all the tough guys I admired growing up in TV, movies, and sports, it was the men who brought their authentic selves who made the greatest impact on me. They didn't seek attention or puff out their chests to prove themselves. They showed that men could cry, feel big feelings, and love their families—not by dominating, but by lifting them up in sacrificial and self-giving ways.

These men's identities were tenderly rooted in a big love that can only come from God. They were role models I have tried to follow of what it means to be a man—to be a father.

Learning How to Be a Man (or Not)

My father was a complicated man—brilliantly gifted with intellect and wickedly funny, with a tender soul and a sensitivity to others. He understood the importance of women being equals, both at home and in the workplace. But he also struggled with mental illness, suffering from deep bouts of depression and bipolar disorder. His unwillingness to address his depression eventually led him to leave our home.

So my view of fatherhood is marked by a duality: memories of a father who loved tenderly but also struggled with his own demons, and the pain of his absence. This complicated reality had a profound impact on me. For a long time, I didn't want children. I was afraid I wouldn't know how to be a good father. It also left me without a mentor to show me what it meant to be a man as I grew into adulthood. My mom did her best to raise me in my father's absence, but a boy needs a father or a male figure to serve as a mirror through which he can discover his own manhood.

Like many boys who grew up in the 1980s and 1990s, I found examples of manhood in tough guys, action stars, professional wrestlers, and athletes. Winning at all costs, saving the day, and being the strongest person were the ideals of manhood that surrounded me.

One memory that stands out is when I was thirteen. My dad had just moved out, and I was struggling to sort through my feelings. Honestly, feelings were not something we dealt with well in my house. A woman who cared for us as children suddenly died of a heart attack. This was a major blow to our family, especially to my sister and me. She had been a constant presence when my parents were either working or fighting, often meeting our emotional needs when my parents could not. Her death, so soon after my father's departure, felt like yet another reminder that those who love you most will eventually leave.

We received the news of her death at the home of a family friend who also loved her dearly. I remember trying to stay tough and not cry while my sister and the others wept. The father of this other family looked at me and said, "Ben, I would think a lot less of you if you didn't cry about this." I did cry, though in a controlled way. Feelings were hard for me then, and they still are. But that moment offered a tiny glimpse of what it means to be taught how to be a man—to be someone who is not afraid of feelings, who is strong enough to be vulnerable, especially when sharing in grief with others.

I've always been a deeply sensitive person. I internalize life and the feelings of others, and it doesn't take much to move me to tears. I was always embarrassed about that. As a kid, the word sissy was thrown around a lot, especially for boys who displayed tenderness.

It stung even more when coaches or adult men referred to boys who showed emotion as sissies. "Don't be a sissy," they would say whenever I felt tears welling up. In my home, we didn't do feelings well—at least not the kind that made us feel vulnerable. We opted for anger instead of admitting fear or hurt.

We often teach our children that toughness is a more admirable trait than sensitivity. Toughness is seen as a sign of strength and resilience, while being sensitive or allowing ourselves to feel deeply is viewed as a vulnerability that undermines our strength. But it's a myth to think that sensitivity and strength are mutually exclusive.

Brené Brown writes, "Vulnerability sounds like truth and feels like courage. Truth and courage aren't always comfortable, but they're never weakness."[1] Real strength, real manhood, isn't found in the moments when we puff ourselves up or try to convince the world we're invincible to pain. It is found in the moments when we dare to be our truest, most authentic selves—embracing life with all its emotions and expressing who we really are.

As I write this chapter, I reflect on a moment from the 2024 Democratic National Convention that moved me as a father. Governor Tim Walz, then the vice-presidential nominee, delivered a speech paying tribute to his family, especially his children. His son Gus, who is neurodivergent, was in the audience and became overcome with emotion, cheering as the convention hall erupted. His face was filled with tears, and he could be seen mouthing, "That's my dad!"

That moment was particularly powerful for me, as it demonstrated two profound visions of true manhood—one of fully embracing our emotions without fear, and the other of being a father who loves and accepts his child exactly as they are, so deeply that the child's love and pride are reflected back, moving them to tears.

There's a lot I could say about true manhood—enough for another book, perhaps. But for me, manhood is something we grow into over the course of our lives. It is best expressed in the ways we

---

1. Brown, *Daring Greatly*, 37.

love—the ways we give of ourselves for the sake of others, whether our spouse, children, community, or even our country. It's a way of being in the world marked by fearless tenderness, an openhearted willingness to offer ourselves and receive others without judgment. It's the cultivation of a strength found in our ability to be authentic and vulnerable as we strive to be the people God made us to be.

Being a father is a uniquely beautiful role that can have a tremendous impact on the next generation. Despite all the tough guys I admired growing up, it was the men who brought their authentic selves that left the deepest impression on me. They didn't seek to be the center of attention, puff out their chests, or dominate others.

These were men who showed that real manhood, expressed in fatherhood, includes the courage to cry, to love deeply, and to lift others up in self-giving ways. They showed me that real strength comes from being tender and loving, grounded in a love that only God can give. They lived a version of manhood that I believe the world needs now more than ever. This is the kind of man I strive to be, and it's where we go next as we embrace healthier roles.

Chapter 7: Accepting Our Vocations Without Giving Up Our Lives

Never get so busy making a living that you forget to make a life.

—Dolly Parton

The Pursuit of Material Gain

JOHN WESLEY URGED PEOPLE to earn all they can, save all they can, and give all they can.[1] Those first two seem to make sense to us—earn and save so we can have all we possibly can in this life. The only problem is that many of us also wedge "spend all you can" into the equation. We believe that earning, saving, and spending will bring us the security we long for. If we just get that car, that house, that boat, those clothes—we'll be happy.

But happiness through material gain is a fluid thing. It's a moving target that shifts based on whatever we feel we lack or feel insecure about at the moment. We might be perfectly content with our home—until we visit a friend's much larger house. Suddenly our once sufficient space seems smaller or less impressive. We may find ourselves pining for a bigger home, convinced that it would somehow make us happier. The same applies to a car

---

1. See Wesley, "Use of Money."

we see or some other "toy" we had no desire for—until we see a friend enjoying it.

Research shows that children can recognize brands at a very early age. These positive brand impressions can last well into adulthood.[2] When I was a kid, it was the Saturday morning commercials for the latest, greatest cereal, toy, or gadget. Nowadays product placement by YouTube influencers becomes the gateway into the wants and desires of kids.[3]

We might think this overgrown desire for more is just a childhood phase—like not knowing when enough sugar is enough. But we spend our lives trying to learn how to self-regulate our desires. Sure, we learn to be polite and mask it better as we grow up. We may not throw tantrums in store aisles anymore, but we still feel that pull deep inside.

We scroll through social media, and the ads reel us in. Or we see the lives of our friends online and covet what they seemingly have. We feel entitled and resentful, experiencing that dis-ease that whispers, "You don't have enough; you need more." We tell ourselves that if we have more, we won't feel that emptiness anymore.

There are two ways to rid ourselves of the uncomfortable feelings caused by our desire for more. One will eventually cost us a lot in the long run, even if it delivers in the short term. The other might cost us more effort initially but will pay dividends over time. We'll explore both in this chapter.

One approach is to work more and more so we can earn more and afford more. The desire to work excessively can become a drug unto itself. It's not just a means to satisfy our wants and wishes; it becomes an end in itself, promising status, purpose, or both.

The other approach is to learn contentment. Contentment requires balance and discipline. It's about knowing when enough is enough, especially regarding the non-material things we value in life. It also takes discipline to maintain that balance and not waver.

Before we can learn contentment, we need to acknowledge our addiction to work. This is not to diminish the value of hard

2. Krashinsky, "Effects of Ads."
3. Livingstone and Rahali, "Written Evidence on Influencer Culture," 4.

work, which is a noble trait. Rather, it's about recognizing when work becomes an idol in our lives. When it takes priority over our kids, our health, or other nonmaterial things we hold dear, we have an addiction. We may claim it's about the financial gain, but deep down, we know it's more than that. It's about the feelings work gives us—power, purpose, or status. In other words, it's a subtle way of choosing ourselves in unhealthy ways over the people and things we love.

Remember the formula for recovery and healing: We must name it, admit our powerlessness over it, confess our need for God's healing grace, and commit ourselves to trust God's will over our own. So let's name that idol and unpack the ways it has deep-rooted control in our lives.

Becoming a Recovering Workaholic

I grew up in a home where the value of work was a top priority in our family culture. My mom worked long, hard hours as an administrator in public health. I learned early on that being a salaried employee often meant doing extra work without extra pay. She accumulated time off only to save it for an early retirement. The "Protestant work ethic" taught me that a great deal of meaning could be derived from proving how hard we could work.

I was around twelve years old when I started working. I wanted something—I can't recall what—and my mom said I would have to earn the money myself. So I began cutting grass. Soon I was helping my cousin with landscaping, and I took on any odd job a teenager could find—most of them outdoors in the sweltering South Georgia heat.

A magical thing happened: whenever I worked, I was rewarded with money, and a deep sense of satisfaction would wash over me. This, I thought, was what being a productive adult was all about.

By the time I turned fifteen, my mom told me I would need to help pay for car insurance if I wanted to drive. Determined to earn the freedom a car would bring, I decided I was done with yard work and found a job indoors at a local pharmacy owned by a family friend. Over the next decade, I worked my way up, pouring myself into whatever the pharmacy needed.

College and graduate school became the gateway from having jobs to pursuing a career. Education was the promissory note ensuring I could do a certain type of work for the rest of my life.

Once I began working in churches, I embraced the rhythms and routines of my profession, pouring myself into the work. Those early lessons about salaried employees doing extra work with no additional payoff other than advancing the mission came back to me. Nobody could outwork me at a church.

It's worth noting that working hard isn't a bad thing. It's admirable, and I enjoy feeling busy, having my mind and body engaged in meaningful tasks. But workaholism is something else entirely.

Workaholism is an addiction to the feelings we get from being busy or making money. It's the gratification we receive from a paycheck, the admiration of others, or the satisfaction of looking at the internal scoreboard and feeling like we've outworked everyone else. It's the sense of superiority we enjoy when we think we've "won" at life by working harder than those around us. At some point, the satisfaction of being engaged in a task gives way to the addictive payoff of comparing ourselves to others.

Time is the only truly valuable commodity we all possess. There are only twenty-four hours in a day, and every human being has a finite amount of time on this earth—some more than others. How we choose to invest that time says a lot about what we truly value in life. As Jesus might remind us, "Where your treasure is, there your heart will be also."[4] If time is our treasure, then our choices about how we spend it reveal our true priorities.

Like any substance or behavior we abuse, workaholism has a cost. Every time we choose work, especially work beyond what is necessary, we must ask ourselves: What are we saying no to in order to say yes to more work?

It might begin as an effort to complete an important task. Gradually, though, our initiative leads us to spend more and more

4. Matt 6:21.

time working. We might be trying to impress coworkers or supervisors, or perhaps we're chasing a promotion that promises long-term financial security for our family. These goals aren't inherently bad, especially if we're working to help and provide for others.

But it's easy to wake up and realize that we're devoting too much of our time and emotional energy to our work. We work for financial freedom, only to become slaves to our jobs and the expectations that come with them. We do more and more, hoping to eventually earn that hard-fought freedom, only to find ourselves on a hamster wheel, running a race that never ends. We won't get off until we choose to set healthier priorities.

Setting Better Priorities

What does it profit us to gain the whole world but lose our souls? Or what can we really give in return for our lives?[5] Jesus poses these questions in response to his call for radical discipleship: "Take up your cross and follow me." Everything in our world tells us to earn, achieve, and hoard, but Jesus calls us to a different way—one of sacrifice and healthier balance, where we cherish the things of eternal value and let go of what offers only momentary profit. As Robert Frost reminds us, "go the way of the road less traveled," and it might "make all the difference."[6] In a world that promotes extreme ways of living—working harder, longer, and more than anyone else—perhaps the less familiar, yet more meaningful road we need to consider is one of health and balance.

One way to start setting healthier priorities is by taking better stock of our lives from the inside out. We often think of life in terms of work and home—a false dichotomy. Our lives don't neatly divide into the stuff we do at work and the stuff we do at home, because there is one common denominator present in both: us. Everywhere you go, there you are.

---

5. Matt 16:26.
6. Frost, "Road Not Taken."

ACCEPTING OUR VOCATIONS WITHOUT GIVING UP OUR LIVES

To become a healthier version of yourself, it's essential to consider the various aspects that make up who you are—emotional, physical, relational, mental, and spiritual. These five elements are always with us, whether at work, at home, or anywhere else. By paying attention to these areas, we can cultivate a more authentic sense of self, rather than feeling like we're one person at work and another at home. Bringing our true and healthy selves into every environment is a significant step toward overall well-being.

Take a moment to reflect on these five areas—how healthy do they feel? Are you honoring your physical needs? How about your relational needs? And what about your mental and emotional health—how are those holding up? Don't forget your spiritual needs, either. It's easy to overlook them, but simply attending worship on Sundays isn't enough to cultivate spiritual health if you're not engaging with that part of your life throughout the week.

A key step toward greater health in all these areas might involve identifying what you need to say no to for a season. Sometimes creating space and setting boundaries is essential to maintaining the alignment your body and soul need for true health. We only have twenty-four hours in a day and seven days in a week, and our time is like a pie—the more we slice, the thinner the pieces. Remember, saying no to something grants more space to say yes to something else. You might say no to a good thing and find it created the margin you needed to say yes to a better thing.

Speaking of margin, that's another gift we all need to claim in our lives. We live in a busy world held together by instant messages, emails, texts, and expectations of constant availability. We bounce from one thing to the next, barely keeping our heads above water. But what if you didn't have to live that way every day? What would change in your life? Would it make a major difference in your mood or even your ability to love others well?

An article in *Inc.* magazine discusses a business expert who found that people often resist creating margin in their schedules because they fear being viewed as lazy. However, she discovered that creating intentional margin in her life paid unexpected dividends. She began to access intuition that supported her decision-making and found a clarity she never had before. Margin, it turns out, is a multiplier. Her creativity and productivity skyrocketed, even though she was technically doing less.[7]

The point is, whether she was doing more or less didn't matter. What mattered was how she felt while doing whatever she was doing. That feeling of vitality versus being utterly drained is often the true measure of whether we consider our day successful. It's not about the results alone. If we're honest, most of us would prefer days, weeks, and months filled with vitality—even if it means a mix of successes and failures—over long stretches of being burned out but consistently achieving. Everything comes at a price, especially our time.

We can't expect others to adapt to our needs and desires for better balance. The world will continue to spin, and people will continue to be people. It's our responsibility to exercise control over the one thing we can truly control in this life—ourselves. We must look within with rigorous honesty and begin to determine the healthiest path forward for our daily lives.

Work Smart, Not Hard

Once we confront the inner demons around working too much and commit to living in a different way—finding balance in our lives—we can explore some practical tools to help us along this healthier path.

We live in an age filled with hacks for productivity. Whether it's the latest app, journal, or book (often on how to use those apps and journals), countless resources promise us a world of ease and efficiency.

But what if our goal in life isn't to be more productive at all? What if productivity is just another idol we chase in our search for deeper meaning? What if we need to rethink our entire approach to productivity?

---

7. Brustein, "How to Add More Margin."

I once heard someone say, "Work/life balance is one of the most overrated things people say they want." At first, I reacted with skepticism. What do you mean seeking work/life balance is the wrong goal? For most of my adult life, I've heard that achieving work/life balance is the ultimate sign of a healthy life. After all, maximizing productivity in a balanced, healthy way seems to be the elusive goal where we could finally have everything we think we want.

But as I thought more about my friend's critique, I began to see the point. No one can achieve perfect balance in life. Something will inevitably take priority at any given moment, throwing off that balance. When a child gets sick, work takes a back seat. When a big work project is due, you may need to temporarily step away from family responsibilities to get the job done. Life is unpredictable, and there will always be moments when one aspect of our lives demands more attention than another. We often end up spending more time trying to achieve work/life balance than actually enjoying life.

Adding more activities to the scale doesn't help either. Saying yes to more things for your kids, more tasks at work, or more commitments to community service doesn't lead to greater balance; it just weighs the scale down further.

Instead of chasing balance, what if we shifted the goal to something more attainable and meaningful?

Life alignment is about arranging our lives so that the things we invest time in genuinely reflect the values we hold most dear. Rather than continuously adding to both sides of the work/life scale, we can focus on removing the non-essential. By clearing away the clutter, we create space to invest deeply in what truly matters and aligns with our core values.

Rule of Life

A rule of life is a concise way of clarifying your priorities and values. It offers a holistic perspective on life, helping you understand

and align both your inner and outer world. Rules of life are meant to be seasonal; as your life evolves, so does your rule.

For example, my "Summer 2024 Rule of Life" was: "I will lead a balanced life where I focus more on the intangible things that bring me joy and rest and ignite my energy and passions. I will not take on new work unless it's fun."

Of course, I continued fulfilling my responsibilities as a pastor, husband, and father. But this rule of life served as a reminder that summer is also a time for rest and renewal. It helped me recognize when it was time to say enough is enough, and embrace my personal limits before taking on too much.

Your rule of life might change as your kids grow up, shift as you progress in your vocation, or take a new shape when you enter a different phase of life. No matter where you are, a rule of life acts as a North Star, guiding you through the season you're in.

Quality over Quantity

How long is your daily to-do list? I used to write lists with ten to twelve items. Of course, I would only check off five to seven tasks and then feel stressed about not finishing the rest. I believed that the more things I could check off, the better I was at being productive. I can't count how many days I stressed myself out over not accomplishing enough.

A funny thing happened around the time I began my life in recovery—I stopped stressing. You know why? I shrunk my list!

Instead of trying to overextend myself daily, I honor my limitations by limiting my to-do list to five to seven items. I might finish them all or add a couple more during the day, or I might only complete three. The point is, naming fewer tasks allows me to be more present while doing them.

I've also learned to measure quality over quantity. Instead of judging my day by how many tasks I accomplish, I focus on being present, of service, or simply aware throughout the day. I purposely build margin into my schedule. Ideally, no meeting ends with another starting immediately after. I take breaks—whether to walk around, breathe, walk the dog, or just sit for five minutes and look out the window. Slowing down like this often leads to a healthier, happier day.

You probably don't need more "balance" in life. Let go of that myth—it has likely contributed to unhealthy perfectionism. Alignment is what leads to greater health: doing what matters, not doing more than we should, and trusting God with the rest.

Chapter 8: Accepting Our Ongoing Soul Work

Listen to your life. See it for the fathomless mystery it is. In the boredom and pain of it, no less than in the excitement and gladness: touch, taste, smell your way to the holy and hidden heart of it, because in the last analysis all moments are key moments, and life itself is grace.[1]

—FREDERICK BUECHNER

Daily Rhythms of Prayer

PRAYER IS ONE OF those things people of faith know they should do, yet often they're not sure how or even why they should do it. It's like eating your vegetables—you know it's good for you, but you're not entirely clear on why or how to consume as much as the experts recommend.

How do you pray, and how often? Is it something you do daily, or something you know you should invest more time in?

I've been a pastor for almost fifteen years and a Christian for most of my life. Yet I have to confess that my prayer life has often been spotty at best. When I did pray, it was more out of a sense of obligation—one of the "shoulds" my perfectionism deemed necessary to live up to all the things I thought were important.

1. Buechner, *Now and Then*, 87.

Learning how to pray is difficult. As children, we're taught to ask God for what we need. That sounds good, but as we grow, those needs often turn into wants, and our prayer life becomes centered on ourselves. We don't quite outgrow the belief that God is a cosmic genie just waiting to grant our every wish. So we go to God in prayer, tossing our requests up like coins in a fountain, hoping for something good in return. It has taken me a very long time to realize that prayer is much deeper, more mysterious, and more complex than that.

Recovery has opened me up to a life of prayer I had never known. Whereas I used to pray mostly for the things I wanted or the pressing concerns on my mind, I've come to experience prayer as something more profound. In recovery meetings, we often recite the AA Serenity Prayer:

God, grant me the serenity to accept the things I cannot change, courage to change the things I can, and the wisdom to know the difference.

I must admit, I had known this prayer for many years and often dismissed it as trite. Its simplicity seemed easy to scoff at, especially as a seminary-trained professional in faith studies. But when I needed to get sober and transform my life from the inside out, that simple prayer began to slowly unleash its power on my soul.

Praying for Acceptance

Serenity is that feeling of being calm, peaceful, and untroubled. For an alcoholic, this state can seem like an unreachable goal. We're uncomfortable in our own skin, filled with inner angst that can feel overwhelming. We hope and pray others won't discover how we really feel. My sponsor likes to say we're just "egomaniacs with an inferiority complex."

You don't have to be an alcoholic to resonate with those feelings. Many of us struggle with self-doubt, feelings of being overwhelmed, and the sense that we're not enough. We worry we're imposters, pretending to impress others and just get by. We all have deep longings and unmet needs that we're unsure how to handle. Who among us doesn't long for the peace of mind that comes with serenity—if for no other reason than to put down the burden of daily worry?

Serenity is born from acceptance. To pray for acceptance is to recognize our limitations. We cannot control people, places, or things; we can only control ourselves and how we react to external forces. A friend in recovery once told me that a meaningful part of prayer is asking to "accept life on life's terms." This means we pray to accept life as it comes, rather than trying to force what we want to happen.

Acceptance is deeply rooted in the perspective we carry about life. How often do we find ourselves worrying about the future or dwelling on the past? The two days we have no control over are yesterday and tomorrow—all we truly have is today.

This doesn't mean we shouldn't be mindful of our past or future, but those things need to be kept in perspective. We should make amends for past mistakes, learn from them, and do the work needed to grow into the future—even if that future is unknown. But ultimately, all we truly have is today—nothing more, nothing less. Each new day is a gift from God, and our task is to live in light of the grace that comes with each day.

Praying for Courage

Out of our acceptance, we can ask God for the strength to address the things we do have the power to control—namely, ourselves and how we show up in each new day. The courage we seek isn't so much about facing external challenges as it is about gaining a clearer awareness of ourselves. It's about recognizing what we can control versus what we can't. Most days, we're not trying to vanquish an enemy, but rather to clear away the ego that clouds our vision and judgment, so we can truly see who we are and what we have power over.

For me, I start with the power I have to work on myself. If I'm angry with someone, I need to focus on my own feelings. I need to name and accept them. Then, I must process them in a way that prevents resentment from taking root. Grudges may feel good in the moment, but they slowly poison our souls over time. If I'm frustrated by an uncertain future, instead of worrying myself to death, I should pray for the ability to accept my current reality and ask God for the willingness to live in it—not in the future I wish would unfold.

It's easy to blame others and hold grudges. It takes real courage to be honest about our feelings and take ownership of our role in working them out.

Praying for Wisdom

It's becoming clearer how vital wisdom is in our lives—the wisdom to recognize what we can control and what is beyond our control. It takes discernment to distinguish between what is real and what is merely a projection of our fears or assumptions. Don't believe me? Think about every conversation you've rehearsed in your mind about a situation that hasn't even happened yet. Think about how often you anticipate the worst outcome in a conflict, already bracing yourself for disappointment or failure. But here's the truth: those things are *not* real if they haven't happened yet!

Wisdom reminds us that we can either dwell on a reality that hasn't materialized, or we can live fully in what is real today, trusting God with the future. I've noticed how my emotional energy gets drained when I fixate on things that haven't occurred. The real peace I seek comes from clarity—understanding what is real today and trusting God with what is not yet real.

The good news is that if this wisdom feels hard to attain, we can start by praying for willingness: *Lord, give me the willingness to trust you when I don't know how.* Slowly but surely, that willingness will come. And wisdom will follow, inch by inch, as we learn to accept our reality and find the courage to do only what we can, trusting God with the rest.

Simple Prayers for Daily Living

I start my day with a simple prayer framework that grounds me: gratitude, submission of my life to God's love and care (step three), asking for freedom from the character defects that keep me from connecting with God and others (step seven), and seeking guidance to live sober, love freely, and let go of my need to control everything. I make sure to include gratitude for being sober for another day and to ask for help to stay sober for that day. I ask God to direct my life and increase my vision beyond myself so I can be of service to someone else that day. All of this is meant to keep the perspective on that given day since that's all we have. I usually pray this prayer in the quiet of the morning while driving to the gym.

On my way home, I reflect in silence. I try to find a moment of stillness where I can rest and be aware of God's presence. It may sound mystical, but it's something anyone can do. It requires quieting the mind, tuning in to the soul, and then listening outwardly to the life that exists in the silence. You can feel the weight of the air, smell your surroundings, and experience a lightness as you settle into this space. That's where God meets us intimately. This way of praying, marked by silent awareness, is just as important—if not more so some days—as my morning prayer filled with words and requests.

Sabbath and Finding Healthy Rhythms

To paraphrase T. S. Eliot's "Burnt Norton," we are to "find the inner place of stillness in a turning world." Dallas Willard observed, "The most important thing in your life is not what you do; it's who you become."[2] The ongoing question we quietly wrestle with is whether we will be frenetic people, consumed by hurry and anxiety, or secure individuals, grounded in our true selves and guided by God as our North Star. Sabbath is a spiritual practice that embodies the answer we long to give to that great question.

---

2. Willard, *Divine Conspiracy*, 361.

Sabbath is traditionally defined as "the seventh day of the week observed from Friday evening to Saturday evening as a day of rest and worship by Jews and some Christians."[3] A theological understanding of Sabbath includes multiple dimensions—rest, worship, covenant, and eschatology—rooted in both the Old and New Testaments.

A healthy life rhythm includes regular Sabbath rest and renewal. A friend once told me, "If God can take a day off during creation, who do we think we are to work seven days a week?" It's a good question. In a world that values maximizing productivity, practicing Sabbath rest can be a profoundly countercultural act.

Observing the Sabbath is about giving up the illusion of control we think we have through constant productivity. It's a regular reminder that God is in control, not us. It's the spiritual practice of surrendering to the truth that God is God, and we are not. When we rest, we witness that the world keeps turning without our hands on the wheel or foot on the gas pedal 24/7. In fact, our lives—and perhaps the lives of those around us—would benefit from us taking a day off, allowing ourselves to let go and let God take charge.

I'm sure the thought of creating such margin in your life feels overwhelming, especially if your daily and weekly rhythms revolve around maximizing productivity. Letting go for a day may seem impossible. But there are ways we can gradually incorporate the spiritual practice of Sabbath into our routines.

One way is to build margin into our daily lives. Do you plan your day with intention? Do you make goals or to-do lists? These are great practices to keep you from feeling tossed around by life's demands. However, as with most things, moderation is the key to maintaining balance.

If you're someone who plans daily or weekly, how full are your plans? Are you scheduling something for every hour? Do you know your to-do list is too long, but feel the pressure to fit it all in? Do you carry the burden of being all things to all people at all times?

---

3. *Merriam-Webster*, "Sabbath."

Incorporating margin into your daily and weekly planning is a great way to practice Sabbath. It creates the breaks we need to prevent burnout and, more importantly, reminds us of our rightful place in God's world. When planning your day, carve out time between tasks to move more slowly. Take a fifteen-minute break after a meeting. Turn off the radio and pray while sitting in the car line waiting for your kids. Walk the dog. Or simply set a timer, stare out the window, and reflect on your day, your life, God's grace, and how you're feeling in that moment.

Carving out an entire day for Sabbath rest is something you can work up to. I have a friend who observes Sabbath every weekend, and he and his family agree to disconnect from their phones for a while. This shift pulls them out of their isolated worlds and devices and into a communal space where they can talk, share, or enjoy activities together. Social media and our devices can become gardens we feel the need to tend 24/7, distracting us from the physical world around us that longs for our presence.

Being intentional is key to building this margin into your daily and weekly rhythms. It means planning ahead, working ahead, and allowing yourself the security to take a break when needed. It also means learning to say no to extra commitments that may consume the margin you've created. Saying no allows you to say yes to rest and renewal. One of the hardest yet most life-giving lessons I'm learning in recovery is that it's better to be really good at a few things than spread too thin and overcommitted to many things. Building rest into my life means I can show up as my best self for the things that matter most.

Learning to Love Yourself

The hardest person you may ever learn to love in this life might just be *you*.

Jesus teaches us to love our enemies and welcome the stranger. This is difficult, but at some level, we know it's essential if we are to reflect the faith we claim. But what happens when that

ACCEPTING OUR ONGOING SOUL WORK

enemy or stranger is not "those people" out there, but the person staring back at us in the mirror?

For most of my life, church has taught me that loving others means learning to love beyond myself. And that's true. But I wonder if we're missing something when we prioritize loving God and neighbor, only leaving whatever love remains for ourselves.

A big part of my recovery is facing the inner turmoil I feel when I don't measure up or when I'm overly critical of myself. The love, forgiveness, mercy, and grace I'm called to extend to others often seem to dry up when it's time to offer them to myself. I wish I were smarter, stronger, more accomplished, or more attractive. Sometimes I wish I were anything other than the person I see in the mirror.

I might say I love God and my neighbor, but the truth is, that love has limits so long as I struggle to love myself. Until I learn to truly love myself, I cannot fully love others in the way Jesus calls me to.

Loving ourselves begins with understanding and accepting the complexities we carry within. The more we understand and embrace who we are, the more we can love ourselves and others.

There is a you who exists in the physical world—the you that people see, hear, and experience. And there is a you that lives in a quieter, inner world—the part of you that remains hidden from others. Think of those times when you outwardly seem fine but are wrestling with conflicting feelings inside. These two "yous" coexist.

Carl Jung is famous for naming this duality. He described the journey of self-realization as the process of becoming aware of and integrating the different parts of ourselves, especially the unconscious elements. This process leads to a unified personality—a "whole self" that is free from the pressure to fit into others' ideas of who we should be.[4]

Children understand this innately. Before they become self-conscious, they live authentically—whether they're happy, sad, or angry, it's clear. The struggle for children is learning self-regulation,

---

4. Storr, *Essential Jung*, 226–48.

while adults often think they've mastered this but have, instead, just learned how to suppress their emotions.

It took me years to recognize the disconnect between my inner self and the version of me I presented to the world. Coming to terms with that disconnect was just the beginning of a journey that led me back to childhood trauma, insecurities, perfectionism, and workaholism—things that alcohol could numb, but only for a while.

What are you hiding from the world?

- A fear of not measuring up?
- Secrets or lies?
- An unhealthy relationship with substances, shopping, attention, or food?
- Anger, resentment, or bitterness?

There may be trauma you're dealing with that needs professional help to process, and I encourage you to seek it. We all carry within us an inner child who once knew themselves more fully. Burying grief and pain will only keep them from healing. That pain may be your grief asking for release and healing.

The child within you longs to be loved, not hidden away. They know you have something special to offer, and they hold the key to unlocking that gift so you can share it with the world.

We often construct an outer life, filtering ourselves to hide the rough edges. But this creates tension that causes us emotional distress. Learning to love yourself means sifting through the mess and becoming empowered to embrace yourself as you are.

Each of us is a child of a loving God, created in the image of the divine. This means we carry within us the image of God—a gift that must find expression in our lives. You don't have to live with the distress of a fragmented self. While it doesn't magically go away, you can, one day at a time, learn to live more fully as the person God made you to be—the truest version of yourself, even the part you think is long lost.

Our inner lives are shaped by many things—hopes, fears, memories, joys, hurts, griefs, and insecurities. Practices like prayer and Sabbath, along with reading Scripture and being active in a faith community, help us sift through these layers. We aren't trying to fix ourselves as much as understand ourselves better. By embracing the good, the bad, and the ugly, we trust God to cover it all with grace—a grace that has the power to unlock levels of love and acceptance we never thought possible.

Chapter 9: Accepting a Life of Service to God, Neighbor, and Self

Life can only be understood backwards; but it must be lived forwards.

—SØREN KIERKEGAARD

Blessed to Be a Blessing (Gratitude)

WHAT IS OUR LIFE'S purpose? It's a big question, but one that can guide us toward the conclusion of this book and, hopefully, the changes you want to embrace in your life.

As babies, our biological wiring tells us that our purpose is to survive. We are helpless and completely dependent on the love and care of others. As we grow, we gradually become more self-sufficient. But even during childhood, we remain in need of love and care to help us navigate the world.

By adolescence and young adulthood, we transition into becoming fully independent. We spend years trying to break away from the need for others as we establish ourselves—getting an education, finding a job, and creating our own place in the world. These milestones aim to cement our independence.

However, even as we achieve independence, we still have a lingering need for love and care—perhaps not as much for our physical survival, but certainly for our emotional well-being. No matter how self-sufficient we try to become, we are never truly independent. We need each other.

Suzanne Simard, a Canadian ecologist, has spent years studying the behavior of trees. In her TED Talk, she explains how trees establish underground root systems to share resources with one another, even across different species. When one tree is sick or in need of more resources, the surrounding trees send help through this underground network.[1]

In other words, trees demonstrate that while survival is essential, it is deeply rooted in interdependence. They thrive through mutual care and support, not isolation. Instead of trying to live independently from one another, we should lean into our interdependence while maintaining healthy boundaries.

Babies teach us that we do not survive without the love and care of a power greater than ourselves. For babies, it's their parents or caregivers. For adults, that power is God. There is nothing we can do apart from the love and grace of God, who sustains and empowers us. This grace is so profound that it fills us with deep gratitude. And it's this gratitude for God's goodness that leads us to our ultimate purpose in life: we are blessed by God so that we can be a blessing to others.

This final chapter is a call to live with the focus and direction God intends for us all—to love ourselves, to love and serve others, and to give ourselves fully and wholly to God.

Freedom in Giving of Ourselves (Service)

Jesus says, "No one has greater love than this, to lay down one's life for one's friends."[2] This can sometimes lead us to believe that our purpose in life is to give of ourselves until we have nothing left. But the spirit of sacrificial giving is more nuanced and complex.

To give ourselves "unto death," as Jesus teaches, is really about finding a healthy balance between giving to others and

---

1. Simard, "How Trees Talk."
2. John 15:13.

caring for ourselves. Giving until we're empty can easily become an act of ego—a performative kind of giving where we seek recognition just as much as, if not more than, the impact of our giving. We've all seen the martyr who loudly proclaims how much they sacrifice. Whether it's time, energy, or emotional bandwidth, they want you to know how busy they are for the sake of others. The problem is, this martyrdom is often framed in terms of busyness—so much sacrifice that there's no rest, no peace.

However, we're not called to give in ways that harm our own well-being. We cannot give what we do not have. If we fail to love and care for ourselves, we can't offer our full love to others. Overworking or busyness, under the guise of self-sacrifice, often comes from a desire to prove our worth or importance. But our true worth doesn't come from our work or from what we give—it comes from God and the fact that we are God's beloved children. We don't have to prove anything to anyone. When we shed those distractions, our giving becomes more authentic and life-giving.

So laying down our lives isn't just about physical dying—it's about a death to our ego. We give not to gain recognition but to truly serve others. As life with God teaches, any good gift is fully realized when we give it away. Gradually our focus shifts from what we gain from giving to the gift itself and the blessing it offers others.

The freedom that comes from this is freedom from the prison of our ego. True freedom is less about personal autonomy and more about the peace we experience when we focus on serving others. We free ourselves from the expectations we think others have of us, or from the burdens we place on ourselves to meet some arbitrary standard of success. In this freedom, we are released to simply be ourselves.

There are three primary assets we can offer others out of this freedom: our financial resources, our emotional resources, and our time.

James tells us, "Every generous act of giving, with every perfect gift, is from above."[3] Our lives are made up of countless gifts

---

3. Jas 1:17.

from God, and our response to these gifts is to share them with others. Jesus says where our treasure is, there our hearts will be also. A look at our bank statement can reveal where our hearts truly lie. If our financial resources are mostly spent on selfish indulgences, it shows what we prioritize. By making space for generosity, we worship God through the act of giving—offering back a portion of what God has freely given to us.

We can also give our emotional resources through how we love others. It's easy to become fixated on ourselves—our needs, our worries, our to-do lists. Entire days can pass with us thinking only about ourselves if we're not careful. One way to break this cycle is to make room for others in our prayers. Perhaps you create a list of people you pray for daily or spend more time praying for the world, your community, or friends in need. Bob Pierce, the founder of Samaritan's Purse, prayed, "Let my heart be broken with the things that break the heart of God."[4] This prayer can serve as a starting point for growing your empathy for the world around you.

Finally, much like our bank accounts, our calendars are a good barometer of how we invest our time. If our schedules are filled only with activities that serve ourselves, it will show. Creating a calendar can become an act of worship. Planning your week intentionally offers space to consider how you might invest your time in service to others. In recovery, one of the best ways to avoid relapse is to focus on others instead of yourself. It broadens our vision, reminding us that God's world is bigger than our narrow view. Serving others becomes a gift that blesses both the giver and the recipient.

Sharing Your Story

Clarissa Pinkola Estés writes, "Stories are medicine. They have such power; they do not require that we do, be, act anything—we need only listen."[5] This resonates deeply with me because stories hold the

---

4. Samaritan's Purse, "Let My Heart Be Broken."
5. Estés, *Women Who Run with the Wolves*, 15.

power to heal. They don't demand anything from us beyond our presence and openness to receive their wisdom. Stories can bridge the gaps between our inner and outer selves, helping us make sense of the world while guiding us toward healing.

In the same way, the Big Book of Alcoholics Anonymous teaches that "nothing will so much ensure immunity from drinking as intensive work with other alcoholics."[6] This principle highlights the transformative nature of sharing our stories and offering support to others on the same path. It's not that people in recovery gain a special power to save others; it's that service shifts the focus of our lives. Instead of being centered on ourselves—our wants, our fears, our addictions—we are called to focus outward, helping others on the same journey.

For alcoholics, the constant goal is securing the next drink—whether it's worrying about supply, manipulating situations to allow for more drinking, or hiding the habit from others. Everything revolves around alcohol. So when recovery begins, the act of sharing our story, of admitting what we have struggled with, feels like stepping into the light after living in darkness.

One of the hardest moments in my life was admitting, "My name is Ben, and I'm an alcoholic." The weight of those words felt enormous. In early meetings, I'd hear others say them so casually, but I couldn't understand how they could carry such a burden so lightly. When I finally spoke the words, I thought I might break down. At first, it was awkward, confusing even. I wasn't sure whether to feel relieved or terrified. Yet each time I repeated the words in a meeting they became easier to say, and I eventually began to believe them fully.

I remember the moment it all clicked. Someone in a meeting shared about how life makes more sense in the rearview mirror. Suddenly I realized that I hadn't craved alcohol in weeks. I had been so focused on just surviving each day without drinking that I missed the miracle when it quietly occurred—God had taken away the intense craving. I left that meeting and cried in my car, overwhelmed by the power of grace.

6. *Alcoholics Anonymous*, 89.

ACCEPTING A LIFE OF SERVICE TO GOD, NEIGHBOR, AND SELF

Your story might not involve alcohol, but it likely involves some form of hurt or struggle. And just as I had to say those words out loud, you can begin your healing journey by naming your hurt: "My name is ___, and I'm hurting from ___." Naming the hurt brings it down to size, rightsizing it within the larger context of your life. It doesn't erase the pain, but it places it into perspective, reducing its power over you.

Your story is complex, and the beauty of it is that it's still being written. With God's help, you can turn the page toward hope and healing. We don't share our stories because we have perfect records of righteousness. We share them because they are the greatest witness we have to the goodness of God. Freely, we have received grace, healing, and love—and we are called to freely give those gifts in return. Our gratitude, service, and stories are offerings of praise and thanksgiving for all that God has done and continues to do in our lives.

We are the gifts God longs to give to the world, and we can begin embracing that truth right now.

A Final Word—For Now

AS YOU'VE MADE IT to this point, you may have more questions than answers about that lingering feeling of existential dread inside. I wish I could tell you that this book offers a quick fix to make everything better in just a few short pages, but it doesn't. What it does offer is a reflection of something I struggle to fully articulate in my own life—the power of God at work in saving me, one day at a time.

I've been part of the church my whole life, and for the last fifteen years I've served in vocational ministry, preaching about God's presence in people's lives each week. But I can honestly say that I've never known the deep truth of that mystery as I have through my journey in sobriety. You may not need to get sober, but we all need to recover from something. My prayer is that this book becomes a starting point for you to discover the saving power of God in your own life, in whatever way you need to find healing and peace. Trust me—I know that's not a small prayer for any of us!

I want to leave you with some words that have become very special for me. These are words spoken in rooms of recovery all over the world on a daily basis. They speak to the heart of what this journey is for me. I pray they speak to you in a powerful way, too:

> If we are painstaking about this phase of our development, we will be amazed before we are half way through. We are going to know a new freedom and a new happiness. We will not regret the past nor wish to shut the

A FINAL WORD—FOR NOW

door on it. We will comprehend the word serenity and we will know peace. No matter how far down the scale we have gone, we will see how our experience can benefit others. That feeling of uselessness and self-pity will disappear. We will lose interest in selfish things and gain interest in our fellows. Self-seeking will slip away. Our whole attitude and outlook upon life will change. Fear of people and of economic insecurity will leave us. We will intuitively know how to handle situations which used to baffle us. We will suddenly realize that God is doing for us what we could not do for ourselves. Are these extravagant promises? We think not. They are being fulfilled among us—sometimes quickly, sometimes slowly. They will always materialize if we work for them.[1]

Sometimes quickly, sometimes slowly . . . God is at work in your life, even right this minute. It's all a mystery. But it's a mystery we can cling to, especially in the most difficult moments of life. We don't have to depend on ourselves to save ourselves—that's God's job.

Thank you, fellow sojourner, for your time and effort—not for reading this book so much as the investment you're making in your own healing. The world will be a better place because of your trust in God. Your journey matters. You matter. Thank you for all you are and all you will become. Amen.

---

1. *Alcoholics Anonymous*, 83–84.

Bibliography

Alcoholics Anonymous. 4th ed. New York: Alcoholics Anonymous World Services, 2001.

Bonhoeffer, Dietrich. *The Cost of Discipleship.* Translated by R. H. Fuller. Revised and edited by Irmgard Booth. New York: Touchstone, 1995.

Brown, Brené. *Daring Greatly: How the Courage to Be Vulnerable Transforms the Way We Live, Love, Parent, and Lead.* New York: Gotham, 2012.

———. *The Gifts of Imperfection: Let Go of Who You Think You're Supposed to Be and Embrace Who You Are.* Center City, MN: Hazelden, 2010.

Brueggemann, Walter. *Sabbath as Resistance: Saying No to the Culture of Now.* Louisville: Westminster John Knox, 2014.

Brustein, Darrah. "How to Add More Margin in Your Day." *Inc.*, Sept. 24, 2023. https://www.inc.com/darrah-brustein/how-to-add-more-margin-in-your-day.html.

Buechner, Frederick. *Now and Then.* New York: HarperCollins, 2010.

Cleveland Clinic. "How to Overcome an Existential Crisis." July 9, 2024. https://health.clevelandclinic.org/existential-crisis.

Estés, Clarissa Pinkola. *Women Who Run with the Wolves: Myths and Stories of the Wild Woman Archetype.* New York: Ballantine, 1992.

Friedman, Edwin. *Generation to Generation: Family Process in Church and Synagogue.* New York: Guilford, 1985.

Frost, Robert. "The Road Not Taken." Poetry Foundation. https://www.poetryfoundation.org/poems/44272/the-road-not-taken.

Guy-Evans, Olivia. "Primary and Secondary Emotions: Recognizing the Difference." Simply Psychology, Oct. 9, 2023. https://www.simplypsychology.org/primary-and-secondary-emotions.html.

Hazelden Betty Ford Foundation. "Forgiveness Is the Art of Releasing Resentment." Nov. 4, 2006. https://www.hazeldenbettyford.org/articles/forgiveness-is-the-art-of-releasing-resentment.

Jung, Carl. *Aion: Researches into the Phenomenology of the Self.* Translated by R. F. C. Hull. Princeton: Princeton University Press, 1969.

Kerr, Michael E., and Murray Bowen. *Family Evaluation: An Approach Based on Bowen Theory*. New York: Norton, 1988.

Kierkegaard, Søren. *Practice in Christianity*. Edited and translated by Howard V. Hong and Edna H. Hong. Princeton: Princeton University Press, 1991.

Krashinsky, Susan. "The Effects of Ads That Target Kids Shown to Linger into Adulthood." *Globe and Mail*, Mar. 13, 2014. https://www.theglobeandmail.com/report-on-business/industry-news/marketing/lovable-marketing-icons-retain-their-power-into-adulthood/article17479332/.

Lamott, Anne. "12 Truths I Learned from Life and Writing." Apr. 2017. TED video. https://www.ted.com/talks/anne_lamott_12_truths_i_learned_from_life_and_writing.

———. *Traveling Mercies: Some Thoughts on Faith*. New York: Pantheon, 1999.

Livingstone, Sonia, and Miriam Rahali. "Written Evidence on Influencer Culture and Children." UK Parliament, Digital, Culture, Media and Sport Committee, Influencer Culture Inquiry. Nov. 12, 2021. https://committees.parliament.uk/writtenevidence/40900/pdf/.

Merriam-Webster. "Rightsize." https://www.merriam-webster.com/dictionary/rightsize.

———. "Sabbath." https://www.merriam-webster.com/dictionary/Sabbath.

Merton, Thomas. *New Seeds of Contemplation*. New York: New Directions, 1972.

NeuroLaunch. "Genogram Emotional Relationship Symbols: Decoding Family Dynamics." Oct. 18, 2024. https://neurolaunch.com/genogram-emotional-relationship-symbols/.

Nouwen, Henri J. M. *The Wounded Healer: Ministry in Contemporary Society*. New York: Image, 1979.

O'Connor, Flannery. *A Good Man Is Hard to Find*. London: Faber & Faber, 2019.

Psychology Today. "Codependency." https://www.psychologytoday.com/us/basics/codependency.

Rohr, Richard. *Falling Upward: A Spirituality for the Two Halves of Life*. San Francisco: Jossey-Bass, 2013.

Samaritan's Purse. "Let My Heart Be Broken by the Things That Break the Heart of God." Jan. 25, 2020. https://samaritanspurse.org/article/let-my-heart-be-broken-by-the-things-that-break-the-heart-of-god/.

Sentell, Eric. "In John 3:16, 'Believe' Means More Than Believe." Koinoia, Feb. 18, 2022. https://medium.com/koinonia/in-john-3-16-believe-means-more-than-believe-b62d350818bc.

Simard, Suzanne. "How Trees Talk to Each Other." June 2016. TED video. https://www.ted.com/talks/suzanne_simard_how_trees_talk_to_each_other.

Storr, Anthony. *The Essential Jung*. Princeton: Princeton University Press, 1983.

Wesley, John. "The Use of Money." Discipleship Ministries, 2020. https://s3.us-east-1.amazonaws.com/gbod-assets/generic/Use-Of-Money.pdf.

BIBLIOGRAPHY

Willard, Dallas. *The Divine Conspiracy: Rediscovering Our Hidden Life in God.* San Francisco: HarperOne, 1998.

World Health Organization. *Global Status Report on Alcohol and Health and Treatment of Substance Use Disorders.* Geneva: World Health Organization, 2024. https://iris.who.int/bitstream/handle/10665/377960/9789240096745-eng.pdf.

www.ingramcontent.com/pod-product-compliance
Lightning Source LLC
Chambersburg PA
CBHW060031180426
43196CB00044B/2373